Reaching Reluctant Young Readers

Reaching Reluctant Young Readers

Rob Reid

ROWMAN & LITTLEFIELD

Lanham • Boulder • New York • London

Published by Rowman & Littlefield
A wholly owned subsidiary of The Rowman & Littlefield Publishing Group, Inc.
4501 Forbes Boulevard, Suite 200, Lanham, Maryland 20706
www.rowman.com

Unit A, Whitacre Mews, 26-34 Stannary Street, London SE11 4AB

British Library Cataloguing in Publication Information Available

Library of Congress Cataloging-in-Publication Data
Names: Reid, Rob, 1955– author.
Title: Reaching reluctant young readers / Rob Reid.
Description: Lanham, Maryland : Rowman & Littlefield, [2017] | Includes bibliographical
references and index.
Identifiers: LCCN 2016048343 (print) | LCCN 2017008556 (ebook) | ISBN
9781442274402 (cloth : alk. paper) | ISBN 9781442274419 (pbk. : alk. paper) | ISBN
9781442274426 (electronic)
Subjects: LCSH: Children—Books and reading—United States. | Preteens—Books and
reading—United States. | Middle school students—Books and reading—United States. |
Children's literature—Bibliography.
Classification: LCC Z1037 .R38 2017 (print) | LCC Z1037 (ebook) | DDC
028.5/50973—dc23 LC record available at https://lccn.loc.gov/2016048343

Printed in the United States of America

For Eau Claire

Contents

Preface

I have worked most of my adult life with young readers of all abilities and interests, and nothing gives me more pleasure than to spark the interest of a reluctant reader. I started as a junior high English teacher, spent a few decades as both a public library youth services librarian and as a youth services state consultant and, for the last twenty years, have been teaching at the University of Wisconsin–Eau Claire, specializing in children's and young adult literature. I also spent time on the road as a storyteller and I've visited classrooms working with children on all aspects of literacy. I take great pride working with reluctant readers, and even if I didn't make all of them lifelong readers (I have followed up on some who have indeed made reading a regular part of their life), at least some read the books I pitched to them.

Over the years, I have used many methods to pique the interests of reluctant readers: storytelling, creative dramatics, music, reader's theater, booktalking, and reading aloud to them. In recent years, I've put more emphasis on these last two methods: booktalking and reading aloud. I've combined them by showing the kids a particular book, reading the author's opening lines, giving my "pitch" (my word for booktalking), and then reading a short stand-alone passage from the book to hopefully "seal the deal." In other words, to get the kids to read the whole book on their own.

There is little on the market in recent years on tactics to use with reluctant readers for this age group. Most of the books published in the last ten to twenty years focus on teen reluctant readers or solely on male readers. It's rare to find a book in the field that provides resources for the female reluctant reader.

Reaching Reluctant Young Readers was designed to profile books that will appeal to this age-level reluctant reader, both boys and girls. The 150 featured books are scripted as booktalk/read-aloud presentations for adults working with kids. This project also lists hundreds of other recommended read-alike titles. At the time of this writing, every book listed was in print and available for purchase from most bookselling vendors. Most public libraries have many of the books, and all libraries can access all of the books through their interlibrary loan services.

I'd like to give a special shout-out to three authors who broke barriers to turn reluctant readers into engaged readers: Jeff Kinney, Barbara Park, and Dav Pilkey. Jeff Kinney wrote the Diary of a Wimpy Kid series that made the concept of the hybrid chapter books even more popular than it previously was. I wrote a book review for the first book in the series and concluded by stating, "This is now the first book I'd give to a reluctant reader." And I got a nice reply from author Kinney himself. Barbara Park made bridge books, books that bridge the gap between easy readers and longer chapter books, more popular with her Junie B. Jones series. Junie is a hit with young readers because of her spunky nature and use of colloquial everyday dialogue versus speaking proper English. And Dav Pilkey created the Captain Underpants series, another form of hybrid chapter book that did wonders to make reluctant readers run for the library shelves.

There are dozens of other wonderful authors inside who can do the same thing for young reluctant readers—make them run for the library shelves.

Acknowledgments

Thanks to:

Shawn Brommer at the South Central Library System, Madison, Wisconsin, for inviting me to speak about reluctant readers at a workshop. It gave me the idea for this book on the car ride home;

Cheyenne Braker, for her research assistance;

my book club group who helped me brainstorm titles;

the L. E. Phillips Memorial Public Library, the Altoona (WI) Public Library, and University of Wisconsin–Eau Claire's McIntyre Library;

my students at the University of Wisconsin, Eau Claire, who shared stories of why they didn't like to read as a child, as well as those students who shared reading success stories;

the staff at the Red Balloon Bookstore, St. Paul, Minnesota, for their help;

Charles, for his support from the beginning; and

the students at the following schools for letting me "pitch" the books to them and also for answering my question, "What book would you give to a friend of yours who doesn't like to read?":

Flynn Elementary School, Eau Claire, WI
Lakeshore Elementary School, Eau Claire, WI
Longfellow Elementary School, Eau Claire, WI
Sherman Elementary School, Eau Claire, WI
South Middle School, Eau Claire, WI

Fairchild Elementary School, Fairchild, WI
Gilmanton Elementary School, Gilmanton, WI
Tainter Elementary School, Rice Lake, WI

Introduction

Who Are the Reluctant Readers?

Children may be reluctant readers because they have an inability to read, something that makes it physically hard for them to read. Other children may be labeled alliterate, because they are uninterested in reading, even though they have the ability to read and may, in fact, have high reading skills. It is this second type of reluctant reader this book addresses, the alliterate child.

Both males and females may be reluctant readers. Most of the focus in the literature is aimed at males. However, some research says otherwise. Nielen et al. (2016) states their research shows little difference between male and female reluctant readers. Anecdotally, I teach college-level teacher education courses where more than 90 percent of my students are female. I have heard from many of them, far more than I would have expected, that they were nonreaders as children.

There are many reasons why children, both boys and girls, may be uninterested in reading:

1. Some children might not be confident in their reading skills. They have the ability but fail to use the skills they have. "Reluctant readers don't believe they can!" (Jobe and Dayton-Sakari 1999).
2. Children's preference of reading materials might be negated by an adult in their life. Once, while working as a children's librarian, I observed an elementary school–age boy show his mother fun books he found in the stacks. She told him to return them all and come back with "good books." She told me she wanted him to read award winners. What books did he pick out but had to return? A book about tarantula spiders, a joke book, a how-to-draw book,

and *Captain Underpants*. What he valued in books was not recognized. I felt that I was watching a reluctant reader being made. While the mother believed award-winning fiction was the best thing for her son, he preferred silly humorous fiction as well as nonfiction books. "Many reluctant readers are not story kids—they are, in fact, information kids" (Jobe and Dayton-Sakari 1999).

3. Children might not connect with the characters in the book they are assigned. They may prefer to find a relatable character to help them learn how to deal with life, to help establish their identity (Baker and Wigfield 1999; Brinda 2011; Gutchewsky 2001).

4. They might be anxious about reading. They see it as a threat (Crowe 1999; Nielen et al. 2016), perhaps because it is associated closely with schoolwork (Brinda 2011). Or they might not see any value of the whole reading experience. "Why would I read when it doesn't count for anything?" (Benning 2014). In fact, because reading is closely related to school activities, many children lose interest in reading between grades 4 and 6 (Brinda 2011).

Criteria for Selecting the Profiled Books in This Collection

I selected mostly middle-grade chapter books. They are aimed primarily for children in upper elementary and middle school. A few picture books that appeal to this age range were also added. I looked for both fiction and nonfiction books that had a good mix of protagonists of both genders. I focused on books published since the year 2000 with the majority of the titles published in the last five to ten years. Many older titles are often out of print and harder to locate. To find some of those older books that might appeal to reluctant readers, check out the "Further Reading" section.

The fifteen categories chosen for this project are categories that children have shared with me as their favorites. The categories include their favorite genres, types of books, and include humor, fantasy, horror, science fiction, superheroes and supervillains, mystery and espionage, outdoor survival, animal stories, sports, biographies, friends and family, and school. A fun, quirky genre I discovered during my research is the last category in the book—books about kids who hate to read. Not something you'll find in the library catalog under subject headings, but one that might win over a few reluctant readers who turn down other genres.

In addition to the genres listed above, there are two types of formats I grouped together. By format, I mean the way the story is presented. Those two formats are graphic novels and novels-in-verse. I define each genre and format in their respective chapter's introduction.

For the books chosen to represent each genre and format, I used criteria set up by the Young Adult Library Services Association (YALSA) of the American Library Association (ALA) for their "Quick Picks for Reluctant Readers" lists.

The following criteria were adapted for grades 3–8 and apply to both the 150 profiled books as well as the several hundred additional recommended titles found throughout the book. Quotes below are taken from the official YALSA "Quick Picks for Reluctant Young Adult Readers Selection Criteria" list (2016):

1. The book should have an appealing appearance including the cover as well as the interior font and amount of white space. If illustrations are added, they should add to the storyline.
2. The writing is clear "without long convoluted sentences of sophisticated vocabulary."
3. The vocabulary is within reason of the target audience's reading level without being "noticeably controlled."
4. The author is able to hook the reader's interest in the first few pages of the book.
5. The plot is straightforward and linear with a minimum of flashbacks. It should not be presented in a nonlinear format, jumping back and forth in time and perspective.
6. The perspective is from a single viewpoint.
7. The reader finds the characters relatable.
8. Many of the above criteria can be adapted to apply to nonfiction books. Nonfiction books should also have attention-grabbing text and visuals without being nonlinear or confusing.

The profiled books listed in *Reaching Reluctant Young Readers* each contain most, if not all, of the above criteria. There are many more wonderful titles out there waiting to be matched with readers. This collection is just the start.

Tips on How to Use This Book

Over the years, I've found that booktalking, giving a short advertisement to "sell" the book, actually works. Once kids hear a short piece about a book, they are more likely to pick it up. I'm also a big believer in reading aloud to all ages. Many articles and studies mention the importance of reading aloud to reluctant readers as one way to help them become engaged readers (Anderson et al. 1985; Ciesla 2016; Erickson 1996; Trelease 2013). I firmly believe that we read to kids to get them to read. Let me repeat that. We read to kids to get them to read.

My method is to read the opening lines of a book to attract a child's attention, using the author's own words. That is followed by a short booktalk, or "pitch," to further entice the youngster. This pitch contains a few quotes from the profiled book. Finally, I've identified short, stand-alone passages from each book to be read aloud and give a better sense of the book to the child. Most selections are less than five minutes in length with a few slightly longer. Hopefully, the author's own words will "seal the deal" and encourage the child to read the rest of the book on his or her own.

For anyone who wants to pitch another book, not found in this collection, to children using this approach, be sure that the opening line or lines are captivating and that you can connect your pitch to those lines. As you develop your pitch, focus mostly on the first section of the book and don't try to tell the whole plot. You are creating a short commercial to interest them to explore the rest of the book on their own. Aim for a conversational tone when crafting the pitch. When looking for a stand-alone passage to read, you'll have to read the entire book first. That time is worth it. While reading, jot down page numbers of sections you believe can be fun for the listener.

If the child listens to your pitch and the reading selection and he or she isn't interested in the book, that's part of the process. Simply try another presentation. And maybe another one after that . . . I'm a big believer in the notion that there's a book for everyone, and it might take a little time to find that book. That's our job, to help the kids find their book.

CHAPTER 1

Humor Hybrid Chapter Books

The Diary of a Wimpy Kid series by Jeff Kinney and the Captain Underpants series by Dav Pilkey inspired the popularity of the "hybrid chapter book," middle-grade books whose illustrations have a more active role than the traditional chapter book. While traditional chapter book pictures simply illustrate what the reader has just read, the hybrid chapter book's illustrations pick up where the text leaves off to continue to tell the story. This is a characteristic more common in picture storybooks and graphic novels. Humor is another essential component of this particular format.

Barnett, Mac, and Jory John. *The Terrible Two*. Illustrated by Kevin Cornell. Amulet, 2015. Gr. 4–6.

First line: "Welcome to Yawnee Valley, an idyllic place with rolling green hills that slope down to creeks, and cows as far as the eye can see."

The pitch: Yes, cows as far as the eye can see. Very prophetic opening to this book set in a community where one often hears cows mooing in the distance. "Yawnee Valley is the cow capital of the United States, this side of the Mississippi, excluding a couple of towns that cheat." Miles is not enthusiastic about cows. Nor is he enthusiastic about moving to Yawnee Valley. He was his old school's biggest prankster, the brains behind "The Ghost Prank. The Missing Front Tooth Prank. Operation: Soggy Homework." Miles makes plans to be the prankster of his new school. On the first day of the school year, however, he finds a car blocking the entrance of the Yawnee Valley Science and Letters Academy. Miles smiles. That is one pretty impressive prank. Then Miles frowns. This school already has a prankster, and a very good one at that. "If Miles wasn't the school prankster, he was nobody."

Reading selection: Read chapter 7. Principal Barkin looks at the students gathered on the lawn outside of school. He asks them, "Who did this?" When nobody speaks, Principal Barkin makes everyone crawl through his car one at a time to get into the building. He vows to catch the prankster. "I WILL BE WATCHING YOU, ALL OF YOU, AND I WILL NOT REST UNTIL I FIND THE CULPRIT." The last kid in line, Principal Barkin's son Josh, asks, "Why didn't you just have all of us go through the back entrance?" The chapter ends with the line: "Principal Barkin stared off at a field of cows in the distance. None of them mooed."

Read-alike recommendations: Principal Barkin is replaced by his stern father in the sequel *The Terrible Two Get Worse* (2016). The third book in the series is *The Terrible Two Go Wild* (2017). *Pickle: The (Formerly) Anonymous Prank Club of Fountain Point Middle School* by Kim Baker (Roaring Brook, 2012) also features school pranksters. Ben's school club, the League of Pickle Makers, is a front for their prank exploits.

Barshaw, Ruth McNally. *Have Pen, Will Travel* (Ellie McDoodle series). Illustrated by the author. Bloomsbury, 2007. Gr. 3–5.

First lines: "Warning: This spy sketchbook belongs to me, Ellie Marie McDoodle. DO NOT READ UNDER PENALTY OF PLAGUE & PESTILENCE! No Mercy."

The pitch: Ellie's real last name is McDougal, but since she loves to draw, the kids at her school call her McDoodle. Right now, she's adding secret entries about her aunt Mug, uncle Ewing, and three cousins, Deanna, Eric, and Tiffie. Ellie thinks "all of the cousins are pains." She and her little brother Ben-Ben are stuck on a weeklong camping trip with the relatives. She writes, "So now I'm trapped in a steel projectile, hurtling down the highway into the Great Unknown with a bunch of control freaks and snotty-nosed brats." Ellie is especially upset with cousin Eric. She calls him a "nose-picking, booger-slurping, bug-infested parasite." Ellie has to work extra hard hiding her sketchbook from him. If he ever reads her book, there will be big trouble. Take for instance, their fourth day of camping in a cabin together. . . .

Reading selection: Read Day 4 of Ellie's sketchbook. Ellie climbs down from the top bunk. Eric left several upside-down stickers on the floor beneath the ladder. "So of course, I step all over them. Not too bad, but when you need to run a half mile to the bathroom in the morning, seconds count." She and Tiffie find Eric at the frog pond. The kids argue and Eric falls into the water. Ellie gets pulled into the pond while trying to help Eric. She freaks out. "The feel—like thick syrup all over you. Warm, like a boatload of elephants peed in it." Eric and Ellie climb out of the frog pond and run to the clean water of the nearby lake. The chapter ends with Ellie writing, "I know what I have to do: I have to go back to the frog pond. It's like getting back up on a horse after it throws you. I don't want to, though."

Read-alike recommendations: Ellie doodles in five sequels: *New Kid in School* (2008), *Best Friends Fur-Ever* (2010), *Most Valuable Player* (2012), *The Show Must Go On* (2013), and *Ellie for President* (2014). The Danny's Doodles series by David Adler is filled with doodle-filled margins. The titles in this series are *The Jelly Bean Experiment* (Sourcebooks Jabberwocky, 2013) followed by *The Squirting Donuts* (2014) and *The Dog Biscuit Breakfast* (2015).

Brallier, Max. *The Last Kids on Earth*. Illustrated by Douglas Holgate. Viking, 2015. Gr. 3–6.

First lines: "That's me. Not the giant monster. *Beneath* the giant monster."

The pitch: Thirteen-year-old Jack lives in a fortified tree house after the Monster Apocalypse has arrived. He deals with zombies, Winged Wretches, Vine-Thingies, the Octo-Beast, the Stone Tower Monster, Tentacle Demons, Sea Monsters, and Blarg, a large monster that has picked up Jack's scent. Jack's new life's mission is to save classmate June Del Toro, who eventually yells at him, "I am no damsel in distress!" Jack reunites with his friend Quint as well as the school bully Dirk, who Jack thinks "came out of the womb with facial hair." When Blarg attacks, the kids defend their tree house with Quint's "Little Hug Monster-Stopping Juice Grenades," a catapult "stocked with crud around town," a razor Frisbee launcher, and the broken baseball bat Jack calls the Louisville Slicer.

Reading selection: Begin reading the middle of chapter 3, with the sentence: "Dirk Savage was the most formidable bully at Parker Middle School." Jack is remembering when the Monster Apocalypse first happened. Dirk was just about to punch Jack for mouthing off when they all heard a scream outside of the bus. "This scream was different. It was a scream of pure horror." The bus was surrounded by zombies. End the selection with the passage: "I remember thinking, 'UM . . . THIS CAN'T BE REAL. IT MUST BE A PRANK. A JOKE. A REALITY SHOW, RIGHT?!?' So I said to Quint, 'UM . . . THIS CAN'T BE REAL. IT MUST BE A PRANK. A JOKE. A REALITY SHOW, RIGHT?!?' But it wasn't. That was it. The Monster Apocalypse had begun."

Read-alike recommendations: In the sequel, *The Last Kids on Earth and the Zombie Parade* (2016), Jack is suspicious when the zombies start disappearing. *Max Helsing and the Thirteenth Curse* by Curtis Jobling (Viking, 2015) is the story of a boy who becomes the target of monsters. Its sequel is *Max Helsing and the Beast of Bone Creek* (2016).

Fry, Michael. *Bully Bait* **(An Odd Squad Book series). Illustrated by the author. Hyperion, 2013. Gr. 4–6.**

First lines: "I was stuffed in my locker. Again."

The pitch: That's Nick speaking. He was stuffed in his locker by the school bully Roy. Nick considers himself "the shortest twelve-year-old on the planet." Roy also picks on Molly Wibble, a "freakishly tall girl," and Karl, the only member of the Safety Patrol. The school counselor makes these three misfits band together to protect themselves against bullies. Mr. Dupree, the weird janitor, tries to help Nick. Nick calls the janitor "hippie weird" and goes on to say, "Hippies are dinosaur versions of skaters." Mr. Dupree's advice is that when a bully picks on you, you have to "bring the crazy."

Reading selection: Read the middle section of chapter 8, beginning with the line: "We saw Roy and his pals, The Future Inmates of America." Roy grabs Nick by the leg and lifts him upside down. Nick hears someone yell, "Bring the crazy." He starts barking like a seal, shows everyone what he ate for breakfast, introduces his "imaginary unicorn ninja assassin," points out body organ parts in the clouds, puts a sock on his head, and talks to the lint that lives in his belly button. Molly and Karl add their own versions of "bring the crazy" and Roy takes off. The three bond for twelve seconds until Karl invites the other two over to his house "for milk and toast and we'll watch my sea monkeys play Twister." End the passage with the line: "Still, it was twelve seconds I wouldn't give back."

Read-alike recommendations: The sequels featuring Nick, Molly, and Karl are *Zero Tolerance* (2013) and *King Karl* (2014). *Justin Case: Rules, Tools, and Maybe a Bully* by Rachel Vail (Feiwel & Friends, 2010) is the diary of a fourth grader dealing with bullies. Its companion books are *Justin Case: School, Drool, and Other Daily Disasters* (2010) and *Justin Case: Shells, Smells, and the Horrible Flip-Flops of Doom* (2012).

Griffiths, Andy. *The 13-Story Treehouse.* **Illustrated by Terry Denton. Feiwel & Friends, 2013. Gr. 3–6.**

First lines: "Hi, my name is Andy. This is my friend Terry. We live in a tree."

The pitch: Andy and Terry live in a tree house. And not any old tree house. Their thirteen-story tree house has a bowling alley, an observation deck, a see-through swimming pool, a secret underground laboratory, a lemonade fountain, a man-eating shark tank, and a room full of pillows, to name just a few of its many features. They also have cool devices like a machine that vaporizes vegetables and another that shoots marshmallows into their mouths. Andy and Terry write and draw books together. The latest deadline to their publisher, Mr. Big Nose, is overdue. There are just too many distractions in their thirteen-story tree house.

Reading selection: Start with the very short chapter 2, "The Flying Cat." Terry, the illustrator, is distracted because he is painting a cat. Andy says, "And when I say, 'painting a cat,' I don't mean he was painting a *picture* of a cat. He was painting an *actual* cat. Bright yellow!" Terry is trying to turn the cat into a canary. He drops the cat over the edge of the tree house and instead of falling, the cat sprouts two wings and flies away. Continue reading chapter 3, "The Missing Cat." We learn that the cat is named Silky and belongs to their friend Jill who lives in the forest with "two dogs, a goat, three horses, four goldfish, one cow, six rabbits, two guinea pigs, one camel, one donkey, and one cat." Finish with chapter 4, "The Big Red Nose." The boys meet their publisher, Mr. Big Nose. He yells at them for being "a LOT LOT LOT behind schedule." Terry's excuse is that he has a long "To Do" list as well as a long "To Don't" list that includes "*Don't* stand under falling piano" and "*Don't* wash my undies."

Read-alike recommendations: Andy and Terry continue to expand their tree house in *The 26-Story Treehouse* (2014), *The 39-Story Treehouse* (2015), and *The 52-Story Treehouse* (2016).

Mack, Jeff. *Clueless McGee*. Illustrated by the author. Philomel, 2012. Gr. 4–6.

First lines: "Dear Dad, It's me, PJ! How come you moved? Did the bad guys find your secret hideout again?"

The pitch: PJ believes his father is a private detective moving from state to state. PJ writes him letters about his life. In the first one, PJ describes falling asleep while chewing gum. He wakes up to find the pillow stuck to his head. His mother tries her best to cut it out but leaves a bald spot on PJ's head. PJ wears a trucker cap to school but his teacher makes him take it off. He manages to hide his bald spot until a drop of water lands on him. Knowing his bald spot is now visible, PJ quickly yells, "AAAGH! It's ACID! Help! I'm melting!" He learns that "a lot of people at this school have no sense of humor." PJ sets out to solve the problem of the school cafeteria's missing mac and cheese. Some of the mac and cheese winds up in Principal Prince's bullhorn. PJ gets mac and cheese all over Mr. Prince's suit and is ordered to clean it up.

Reading selection: Read chapter 4, "The Wet Pants Letter." PJ hides Mr. Prince's suit in his refrigerator until his mom complains about the smell. We are introduced to Mr. Toots, the school janitor, who goes around telling everyone, "Don't touch it!"—no matter what "it" is. "Like one time, when Taylor Schmidt threw up in front of the art room, Mr. Toots stood right next to the puddle, saying, 'Don't touch it! Don't touch it' to every kid who walked by." PJ sneaks Mr. Prince's suit into the washing machine and notices the "Dry Clean Only" label on it. "I put the suit in the dryer and pressed Super Dry." Of course, the suit shrinks. PJ complains, "It should have said WET CLEAN ONLY." The chapter ends with PJ yelling, "I'm doomed. DOOMED!"

Read-alike recommendations: There are two more books in the series: *Clueless McGee and the Inflatable Pants* (2013) and *Clueless McGee Gets Famous* (2014). *The Sandwich Thief,* written by André Marois and illustrated by Patrick Doyon (Chronicle, 2016), features a kid named Marin who tries to solve the case of missing food in school.

Moss, Marissa. *The Name Game!* (Daphne's Diary of Daily Disasters series). Illustrated by the author. Simon & Schuster, 2011. Gr. 3–5.

First lines: "Daily Disaster, Thursday: 1. Stepped in dog poop."

The pitch: Daphne Davis is keeping a Diary of Doom, recounting one disaster after another. On the first day of fourth grade, Daphne's teacher accidentally calls her "Daffy." The teacher immediately apologizes but "the damage was done. For the rest of the day everyone called me Daffy. For the rest of my life, I bet." Daphne tries to give the other students nicknames. Vince becomes "Blintz," Lester is now "Pester," and Stephanie's new name is "Stuffy." The plan doesn't work. At the end of the day, Daphne is home with her mother and twin brothers Donald and David. She can only tell them apart because David always has a "green bubble of snot" hanging out of one nostril. "I say it's just disgusting, but it's the only way we can tell David from Donald. We need that Booger Bubble!" Mom asks Daphne if she likes her new teacher.

Reading selection: Read seventeen pages into Day One of the diary, starting with the lines: "Do I like my teacher? Is *she* my enemy? Apart from hating her for getting my name horribly, disastrously wrong, I'm not sure." Daphne describes the ingredients of a terrible teacher. These include giving too much homework or too many tests, being boring, or having an "impossible-to-understand strong accent." Some terrible teachers share too much personal information. Read the doodle word balloon where an imaginary teacher says, "I got food poisoning and spent all day and night on the toilet, emptying out one end or another." The worst teachers are mean teachers. Daphne draws a vampire teacher going, "Bwaahaa haaaa!" End the passage with the sentence: "But she's in her own category, the Can't-Ever-Get-Your-Name-Right one."

Read-alike recommendations: There are two more books in the Daphne's Diary of Daily Disasters series: *The Vampire Dare!* (2011) and *The Fake Friend!* (2012). *From the Notebooks of a Middle School Princess* by Meg Cabot (Feiwel & Friends, 2015) is not heavily illustrated, but is the story of another student keeping track of school disasters in a diary. Its sequel is *Royal Wedding Disaster* (2016).

Pastis, Stephen. *Mistakes Were Made* **(Timmy Failure series). Illustrated by the author. Candlewick, 2013. Gr. 4–6.**

First line: "It's harder to drive a polar bear into somebody's living room than you'd think."

The pitch: The polar bear's name is Total. He wandered 3,101 miles from the Arctic to Timmy Failure's backyard. At least, that's what Timmy tells us. Timmy is the head of Total Failure, Inc., a detective agency. He makes Total the polar bear his partner. Timmy knows he is an ace detective. When Jimmy Weber's house is "TP'd" (covered with toilet paper), Timmy notices an important clue while visiting Molly Moskin's house. Her bathroom has toilet paper. Therefore, Molly Moskin must be guilty. Here's another example of Timmy's "clear-headed judgment."

Reading selection: Read chapter 2, "The Candy Man Can't 'Cause He's Missing All His Chocolate." Timmy takes on the case of Gunnar's missing Halloween candy. Gunnar's little brother is Gabe. As Timmy passes Gabe's room, he sees that "Gabe is sitting on his bed, surrounded by candy wrappers. There is chocolate smeared all over his face and an empty plastic pumpkin on the floor." Timmy writes down the following clue: "Gabe: not tidy." Move on to the one-page chapter 6, "It Ain't Me, Gabe." Timmy returns to the scene of the crime and interviews Gabe. When asked where he was on the night of the crime, Gabe says he was eating candy. Timmy writes: "Can't be Gabe. He has alibi."

Read-alike recommendations: The other titles in the Timmy Failure series include *Now Look What You've Done* (2014), *We Meet Again* (2014), *Sanitized for Your Protection* (2015), and *The Book You're Not Supposed to Have* (2016). *Captain Coconut and the Case of the Missing Bananas*, written by Anushka Ravishankar and illustrated by Priya Sundram (Tara, 2015), features another "clever" problem solver.

Peirce, Lincoln. *Big Nate in a Class by Himself* **(Big Nate series). Illustrated by the author. Harper, 2010. Gr. 3–6.**

First line: "She could have called on anybody."

The pitch: She, Nate's teacher Mrs. Godfrey, calls on Nate to answer a question. Nate says, "Ummm . . . *Koff!* What was the question again?" Nate thinks middle school is "a building that smells like a combination of chalk dust, ammonia, and mystery meat." He gives grades to the different kinds of school days. Field Trip days earn an A+, Substitute Teacher days get a C–, and Normal days earn a D. Train Wreck days are the days when teachers scream at you, they give quizzes or tests, or you get after-school detention. They should be graded with an F. Nate feels he's destined for greatness. He gets a fortune cookie fortune that reads: "Today you will surpass all others." Nate is very upbeat about the new school day. If only he could figure out what the fortune means.

Reading selection: Read chapter 8. Nate and his friends are heading to the school "cafetorium." Nate sees Chad reading *The Complete Book of World Records.* Nate decides his fortune means he will break a world record. Should it be for the longest fingernails? The most tattoos? Nope, Nate is going for "speed eating." Since nobody ever eats the school's green beans, Nate's friend Francis gathers a huge pile of them. Nate, his mouth full of green beans, spits them out and the kids all go, "EEWWWWW!" Nate says, "Okay, relax, people. It's not all THAT gross. A pile of chewed-up green beans looks about the same as a pile of UNchewed green beans." The principal slips on slimy bean juice and Nate is ordered to his office. The chapter ends with Nate saying, "Lucky me. He's alive. And now I REALLY don't feel so good."

Read-alike recommendations: Nate returns in *Big Nate Strikes Again* (2010), *Big Nate on a Roll* (2011), *Big Nate Goes for Broke* (2012), *Big Nate Flips Out* (2013), *Big Nate in the Zone* (2014), *Big Nate Lives It Up* (2015), and *Big Nate Blasts Off* (2016). *The Detention Club* by David Yoo (Balzer + Bray, 2011), is the story of a student named Peter who decides that landing a seat in detention is the key to popularity.

Russell, Rachel Renée. *Tales from a Not-So-Fabulous Life* (Dork Diaries series). Illustrated by the author. Aladdin, 2009. Gr. 5–7.

First line: "Sometimes I wonder if my mom is BRAIN DEAD."

The pitch: According to Nikki's diary, "The drama started this morning when I casually asked if she would buy me one of those cool new iPhones that do almost everything." That would assure Nikki a spot in the CCP: the Cute, Cool & Popular group at the Westchester Country Day School. Because, apparently, having an uncool phone "can totally RUIN your social life." When Mom buys her daughter a diary instead, Nikki has "irrefutable evidence she IS, in fact, CLINICALLY BRAIN DEAD!!" The only way her family can afford this particular school is because of her father's extermination service school contract. Being cool is hard. Nikki prays no one sees her show up "in his work van with the five-foot-long plastic roach on top." And now, instead of the latest cell phone, Nikki has a diary. Only dorks write in diaries. All the cool people blog their juicy stuff online. Nikki vows to "not write in this diary again. NEVER! EVER!!" Of course, she does.

Reading selection: Read the diary entry for Tuesday, September 3. Nikki is assigned to read *A Midsummer Night's Dream* for class. She's surprised Shakespeare "wrote teen chick lit." Her family tries to help her feel better about herself. "Like sticky notes with corny sayings on them will solve my problem of being a TOTAL LOSER at school." The chapter ends with Nikki writing, "I wonder if you still have to hand in homework when you're locked up in a PSYCHO WARD?" Move on to the entry for Friday, September 6. Nikki writes about the peculiarities of "those really expensive teen shops at the mall" where the salesgirls have "their nasty habit of unexpectedly snatching open the curtain of your dressing room and popping their head inside when you're like HALF NAKED." Nikki ends her entry with the lines: "I'm also going to wear a hat, wig, sunglasses, and phony mustache so no one will recognize me. WHATEVER!!"

Read-alike recommendations: Nikki continues to write in several more volumes of her diary including *Tales from a Not-So-Popular Party Girl* (2010), *Tales from a Not-So-Talented Pop Star* (2011), *Tales from a Not-So-Graceful Ice Princess* (2012), *Tales from a Not-So-Smart Miss Know-It-All* (2012), *Tales from a Not-So-Happy Heartbreaker* (2013), *Tales from a Not-So-Glam TV Star* (2014), *Tales from a Not-So-Happily Ever After* (2014), *Tales from a Not-So-Dorky Drama Queen* (2015), *Tales from a Not-So-Perfect Pet Sitter* (2015), and *Tales from a Not-So-Friendly Frenemy* (2016).

Surovec, Yasmine. *My Pet Human*. Illustrated by the author. Roaring Brook, 2015. Gr. 3–4.

First line: "I'm a lucky cat."

The pitch: Why does it seem as though cats are calling the shots? One reason is that they have developed "the Look." That certain "weepy, doe-eyed look" designed to make humans give cats whatever they want. One day, a stray cat spots a human girl eating a bowl of macaroni and cheese topped with tuna. "I must get my paws on that!" it thinks. The cat decides to move in with the girl and her mother who is a "little bit more, um, unfriendly."

Reading selection: Read the majority of chapter 3, "How to Train a Human." The cat is trying to decide if it will live with the humans. The girl is easy to train. "When all else fails, I give her 'the Look.'" The mother is a different story. "The mom is a bit more . . . challenging. Older humans tend to be set in their ways. She's no fun at all. She tends to bark orders. And she gets annoyed easily. But I can change that. With a little time and patience, I can get any human to warm up." One of the cat's strategies is to show the mom how good a hunter it is. "I give her a present from my daily adventures as an expert domestic hunter." The cat brings home a live snake who at one point says, "Er, can I stop pretending to be dead now?" End the passage with the lines: "No one can resist my magical belly. Not even grumpy humans."

Read-alike recommendations: The Bad Kitty chapter books, written and illustrated by Nick Bruel, also feature an independently minded cat in a similar visual format. These titles include *Bad Kitty Gets a Bath* (Roaring Brook, 2008), *Happy Birthday, Bad Kitty* (2009), *Bad Kitty vs. Uncle Murray* (2010), *Bad Kitty Meets the Baby* (2011), *Bad Kitty for President* (2012), *Bad Kitty School Daze* (2013), *Bad Kitty Drawn to Trouble* (2014), *Puppy's Big Day* (2015), and *Bad Kitty Goes to the Vet* (2016).

Tatulli, Mark. *Desmond Pucket Makes Monster Magic.* **Illustrated by the author. Andrews McMeel, 2013. Gr. 4–6.**

First lines: "'Mom! Mo-o-o-o-o-o-mmmm . . .' I groan in my best I'm-about-to-blow-chow voice."

The pitch: When Desmond's mother comes to check on her son, he spits blood and an alien bursts out of his chest. Instead of freaking out, his mother complains, "Are those the new pajamas I just bought you?" and leaves his bedroom in a huff. She knows her son too well. He loves to create special effects. Desmond claims he's "a Professor of Frightology, with a Master's in Monsters." He dreams of creating great amusement park haunted house rides to go along with his monster effects. Desmond loves to torment his sister Rachel. He once transformed her Little Mermaid into a Little Mummy. Desmond is aware that most grownups don't appreciate his talents, especially teachers. They can't prove he's the one behind the pranks, but they have their suspicions.

Reading selection: Read chapter 4, "Desmond's Greatest Hits." He brags that one of his greatest moments was "the shrieking rubber goblin in the teacher's lounge toilet." It was Mrs. Rubin who discovered the goblin. He goes on to say, "It was pretty obvious why Mrs. Rubin was the chorus teacher." Desmond also created the bloody cakes in Home Ec that were used for a Back to School Night event and the giant worms served in the school cafeteria's mashed potatoes. He'd love to take credit for these pranks. However, if he did, he'd get kicked out of school. "Cloverfield Memorial Junior High has a 'zero-tolerance' policy . . . which means that the teachers have zero tolerance for goblins in their toilets and worms in their taters." The chapter ends with a description of Mr. Needles, who suspects Desmond is the one behind the pranks. "And nobody wants to prove it more than Mr. Needles."

Read-alike recommendations: Desmond returns in *Desmond Pucket and the Mountain Full of Monsters* (2014) and *Desmond Pucket and the Cloverfield Junior High Carnival of Horrors* (2016). Although not filled with illustrations, the book *The Big One-Oh* by Dean Pitchford (Putnam, 2007) is about a boy who wants a special effects monster-themed birthday party.

Vernon, Ursula. *Dragonbreath.* **Illustrated by the author. Dial, 2009. Gr. 3–5.**

First lines: "The sea was calm . . . but then the silence was broken by the fearsome sound of pirates! ARR! ARR! ARR? SCURVY!"

The pitch: Mornings are not Danny Dragonbreath's strong point. His alarm clock interrupts his pirate dream. He staggers down to breakfast where his father fixes bacon by breathing "a tiny puff of flame on it. It sizzled." Late bloomer Danny is sad because he can't breathe fire. His father encourages him by saying, "Think hot thoughts." Despite thinking about deserts, firecrackers, and jalapeno peppers, "all he got was a vague ashy taste in his mouth." Sometimes Danny can manage a little smoke, but even gargling with kerosene doesn't help.

Reading selection: Read most of the chapter titled "Food Fight," beginning with the line: "'What took you so long?' asked Wendell as Danny trudged into the cafeteria, holding his tray." Danny's school potato salad is real nasty. The salad even grabs Danny's fork. There's an instructional insert warning that potato salad can "skeletonize a cow in under two weeks, assuming the cow doesn't get bored and move." The school bully, a Komodo dragon named Big Eddy, teases Danny for not being able to breathe fire. He steals Danny's lunch, which turns out okay because "after a few minutes, there was a scream from across the lunchroom. It was the exact sound that a young Komodo dragon might make when he has just been stabbed in the hand with a plastic fork by a plate of recalcitrant potato salad."

Read-alike recommendations: There are several sequels including *Attack of the Ninja Frogs* (2010), *Curse of the Were-Wiener* (2010), *Lair of the Bat Monster* (2011), *No Such Thing as Ghosts* (2011), *Revenge of the Horned Bunnies* (2012), *When Fairies Go Bad* (2012), *Nightmare of the Iguana* (2013), *The Case of the Toxic Mutants* (2013), *Knight-knapped!* (2015), and *The Frozen Menace* (2016).

Watson, Tom. *Stick Dog*. Illustrated by the author. HarperCollins, 2013. Gr. 3–6.

First lines: "This is Stick Dog. He is not called Stick Dog because he likes sticks. Although, now that I think about it, he does like sticks."

The pitch: Stick Dog is called Stick Dog because the narrator can't draw real dogs. Think about how one draws stick people. The narrator says, "I do the same for dogs." He draws four dog friends for Stick Dog and names them Mutt, Stripes (who is actually a Dalmatian), Karen, and Poo-Poo. "Now, it's important to know that Poo-Poo is not named after, you know, going to the bathroom. He's named after his own name. Get it? POO-dle." The dogs spend the entire book trying to steal hamburgers from a family grilling in the park. That might sound boring, but as one "critic" says on the book's back cover, the story will "blow milk out of our noses."

Reading selection: Read chapter 8, "D-I-Z-T-R-A-K-S-H-U-N." Stick Dog's plan to steal the hamburgers is to create a distraction. The other dogs don't know what the word "distraction" means. Mutt thinks it's a small bird, Poo-Poo thinks it's what you do when you lie around ("'You're thinking of "inaction,"' said Stick Dog"), Stripes tries to spell the word (see the title of this chapter), and Karen confuses it with the word "contraction" ("A distraction is when you combine two words with an apostrophe"). Stick Dog is impressed that Karen knows the definition of "contraction." Poo-Poo comes up with the best plan to distract the family. "I can run face-first into a tree and only get hurt a little bit."

Read-alike recommendations: Stick Dog and his friends continue to search for food in *Stick Dog Wants a Hot Dog* (2013), *Stick Dog Chases a Pizza* (2014), *Stick Dog Dreams of Ice Cream* (2015), *Stick Dog Tries to Take the Donuts* (2016), and *Stick Dog Slurps Spaghetti* (2016). A cat named Stick Cat gets his own book in *A Tail of Two Kitties* (2016).

Zemke, Deborah. *My Life in Pictures*. Illustrated by the author. Dial, 2016. Gr. 3–4.

First lines: "The book you're holding in your hands is my life. I draw pictures of EVERYTHING in it."

The pitch: Beatrice Holmes Garcia is an artist. She draws pictures of her favorite things, like stars to make wishes on and her dog Sophie. She also draws some not-favorite things, like waking up to go to school, and her younger brother Pablo, who she calls the Big Pest. Bea's best friend is her next door neighbor Yvonne. They do everything together, like draw pictures, play imagination games in a big tree, and count their Halloween candy. "I have 4 Choco Drops + 9 boxes of Hot Dots + 10 Twirls + 5 Lemon Blasters + 5 Peanut Barks = 33 Treats!" Bea is devastated when Yvonne moves away and a monster moves in next door. Well, at least what Bea calls a monster.

Reading selection: Read chapter 6, "Meet Your New Neighbor." The doorbell rings and the new neighbors show up to say hello. Bea and Pablo meet "the monster," a boy named Bert. Pablo mistakenly calls him "Burp." Pablo thinks it's "funny when Bert stuffed five cookies into his mouth. And burped." Pablo doesn't think it's funny when Bert makes a scary face and scary noises. Bert scares Pablo and the dog Sophie. Bea says, "He didn't scare me. He just made me mad. Really mad." Bea feels rotten, especially when Bert scares Sophie up into the tree so that Fireman Dave has to rescue her. The chapter ends with Bea writing a letter to Yvonne, ending it with the line: "I WISH YOU DIDN'T MOVE AWAY!"

Read-alike recommendations: Two more books that deal with moving and kids who like to draw are *Doodlebug: A Novel in Doodles* by Karen Romano Young (Feiwel & Friends, 2010) and its sequel *Stuck in the Middle (of Middle School): A Novel in Doodles* (2013).

CHAPTER 2

Graphic Novels

Graphic novels use sequential art, a combination of text, panels, and images. The format has grown more popular with young readers over the years and there are many more choices for elementary- and middle-school-age children today. Closely related to comic books, graphic novels are looked down on by some adults as dumbed-down literature, but many reading experts agree these books are very effective for reluctant readers.

Burks, James. *Bird & Squirrel on the Run!* Illustrated by the author. Graphix, 2012. Gr. 3–5.
First line: "What a perfect day for flying!"

The pitch: Bird is enjoying life until he is attacked by a large, scary orange cat. Squirrel accidentally saves Bird by unloading his winter's supply of acorns on the cat. Now Squirrel has no food for the winter, and he is convinced he's facing certain death. The slightly injured Bird tells Squirrel to come south with him for the winter. "We can fly there . . . ow . . . together. Ooh . . . Ahh . . . Well, we can walk there together." Squirrel packs his possessions in a bike trailer and loses it all when Cat attacks again. All three—Bird, Squirrel, and Cat—go over a waterfall.

Reading selection: Start reading on page 42 where Bird says, "That was incredible!" Squirrel laments the loss of his things. Bird finds Squirrel's toothbrush. It is full of green gunk. Bird tosses it aside and says, "Okay . . . but don't blame me when you get cavities." Cat washes ashore, sees the toothbrush, eats it, and is back on the hunt. When Bird and Squirrel seek shelter from a rainstorm, Bird invents a theme song. "Bird and Squirrel! Bird and Squirrel! Two best friends named Bird and Squirrel! I'm a Bird! You're a Squirrel! Bird and Squirrel!" Cat shows up and Bird offers to put him in the theme song. Bird and Squirrel run away and fall into a hole where they are welcomed by Mole. Grandma Mole warns them about cats having nine lives. She also predicts "danger lies ahead."

End the selection on page 67 where Mole says, "Have a safe journey." Flip one more page where we see Cat lurking in the background.

Read-alike recommendations: There are two more books featuring Bird and Squirrel: *Bird & Squirrel on Ice* (2014) and *Bird & Squirrel on the Edge!* (2015). *Gary's Garden*, written and illustrated by Gary Northfield (Scholastic, 2016), is a graphic novel featuring whacky birds, squirrels, caterpillars, spiders, ladybugs, and other creatures.

Camper, Cathy. *Lowriders in Space*. Illustrated by Raul Gonzalez. Chronicle, 2014. Gr. 4–7.

First lines: "Wake up, Lupe! Wake up, Elirio! Wake up, Chavo!"

The pitch: Lupe Impala (a wolf) is a great mechanic. "She could rescue a dropped gasket, notch a belt, or electrocharge a spark plug, swish a swashplate, or wrangle a

manifold with a twist of her wrench and a flick of her wrist." Elirio Malaria (a mosquito) is a wonderful detail artist and Chavo "Flapjack" (an octopus) is an expert in cleaning and polishing cars. The three dream of operating their own garage. They spot a poster advertising the Universal Car Competition where the "most mechanically inventive, exquisitely detailed cosmic car" wins a carload of cash. They themselves are short on *dinero* but start with a junker that's "already low and slow. So slow, it didn't even go." While scrounging around, they find a box of rocket parts and soon their lowrider blasts into outer space. "Low and slow, bajito y suavecito."

Reading selection: Start reading page 38 with the line: "When they were done, the car was ready to drive." The trio find themselves in space. Chavo says, "I don't think we're in the barrio anymore!" They customize their car with the glow of the northern lights, the flames of the sun, meteors for blazing headlights, and the rings of Saturn for pinstripes. To make the car hop, they combine light moondust with heavy gas from Jupiter. Finish the selection where the lowrider is heading into a black hole with the lines: "I can't turn out of the way! It's sucking us in! We're gonna die!"

Read-alike recommendation: Lupe, Elirio, and Chavo return in *Lowriders to the Center of the Earth* (2016). *Space Dumplins*, written and illustrated by Craig Thompson (Scholastic, 2015), is a graphic novel featuring the financially strapped Violet who heads into outer space to save her father.

Hale, Nathan. *Donner Dinner Party* (Nathan Hale's Hazardous Tales series). Illustrated by the author. Amulet, 2013. Gr. 4–7.

First lines: "Hear ye! Hear ye! Hear ye! Let it be known that on this day, this man is sentenced to die by hanging!"

The pitch: Nathan Hale, the historical figure, not the author, the guy who died for America and said, "I regret that I have but one life to give for my country," that guy, is a storyteller in this book. He puts off his execution by regaling the hangman and a British officer with a story that happens in their future: the story of the Donner Party. For those not familiar with that story, travelers resorted to cannibalism in order to survive. In 1846, the Reed family left Springfield, Illinois, with the Donner family to travel to California by wagon train. They were later joined by other families. They left the well-traveled Oregon Trail and sought out a shortcut called the Hastings Cutoff. Bad decision. At one point, Nathan Hale talks directly to us, the reader, and warns, "The next part of this tale is not for the faint of heart. Horrible things are going to happen. If you are easily upset, you may want to skip ahead."

Reading selection: Read the end of chapter 11 beginning with the lines: "Oh, strife! The axle's busted!" The party of travelers is high in the Sierra Nevada. They wake the next morning covered in snow. Their guides cut a trail up a high pass and then return for the others. The party refuses to travel in the dark. They are warned, "You don't understand. If any more snow falls, we'll be trapped up here for good!" The others still refuse to move. They say, "With any luck, the snow won't fall tonight." Show the first picture of chapter 12, a scene where snow is falling through the night.

Read-alike recommendations: The other books in the Nathan Hale's Hazardous Tales series are *One Dead Spy* (2012), *Big Bad Ironclad!* (2012), *Treaties, Trenches, Mud, and Blood: A World War I Tale* (2014), *The Underground Abductor: An Abolitionist Tale about Harriet Tubman* (2015), and *Alamo All-Stars* (2016).

Hale, Shannon, and Dean Hale. *Rapunzel's Revenge.* Illustrated by Nathan Hale. Bloomsbury, 2008. Gr. 4–7.

First lines: "Once upon a time, there was a beautiful girl. That's me there. I lived in a grand villa . . . with loyal servants . . . tasty food . . . and my mother. Or who I *thought* was my mother."

The pitch: Remember the story of Rapunzel? The girl with the really, really long hair who was locked in a tower by a witch? This is her story, but kind of updated. Part of it is set in the Wild West. Rapunzel learns that the person she thought was her mother, Mother Gothel, stole Rapunzel from her real mother. Her real mother is now a slave working for Mother Gothel in the mines. Rapunzel rebels against Mother Gothel and winds up in a giant tree. Mother Gothel has magical powers to control plants, and she plans to take over the whole world. Rapunzel is stuck in the tree tower for years. Long enough for her hair to grow really, really, really long.

Reading selection: Read the last part of chapter 1, "Once upon a Tower," beginning with the lines: "The last time Mother Gothel visited was my sixteenth birthday. Happy birthday to me." Rapunzel uses her hair to escape from the tree tower. When she lands, she is attacked by a giant boar. Rapunzel uses her hair to lasso the boar. A young hunter shoots the boar. Instead of thanking him, Rapunzel sends the obnoxious hunter on his way. She sets off to rescue her real mother. "This is where the 'once upon a time' part ends," she says. Rapunzel adds, "And along the way, I had a thought to teach Mother Gothel that she can't be a bully without earning a swift kick in the rear."

Read-alike recommendation: Rapunzel's companion in *Rapunzel's Revenge* is Jack, from "Jack and the Beanstalk" fame. Their stories continue in *Calamity Jack* (Bloomsbury, 2010) where the two face a giant known as Blunderboar.

Harper, Benjamin. *Hansel & Gretel & Zombies* (Far Out Fairy Tales series). Illustrated by Fern Cano. Stone Arch, 2016. Gr. 4–6.

First line: "Once upon a time, in a distant corner of the Magical Forest . . . there was a lifeless graveyard."

The pitch: Someone took that adult classic book *Pride and Prejudice* and added zombies to it. Someone else took President Abraham Lincoln's life story and added vampires. It's time for young readers to have their turn. The author and illustrator of this graphic novel took that old folktale about the two kids who found a witch's cottage of candy and "zombie-fied" it. Hansel and Gretel are zombie kids who live in a graveyard in the Magic Forest with their zombie parents. They are all starving because there are no tourist brains to eat.

Reading selection: Read the first half of this short, fast-paced book. Mr. and Mrs. Undead put makeup on their children Hansel and Gretel and send them out to find brains. A witch spots the two kids and, thinking they are human, flips her home into one made of baked goods. She's shocked to learn the siblings don't like candy. End the reading when the witch asks, "Then for witch's sake, what DO you like to eat?" In response, the Hansel and Gretel zombies leap at her yelling, "BRRAAINS!"

Read-alike recommendations: The other graphic novels in the Far Out Fairy Tales series include *Ninja-rella* by Joey Comeau and illustrated by Omar Lozano (2015), *Red Riding Hood, Superhero*, written and illustrated by Otis Frampton (2015), *Snow White and the Seven Robots* by Louise Simonson and illustrated by Jimena Sanchez (2015), *Super Billy Goats Gruff* by Sean Tulien and illustrated by Fern Cano (2015), *Jak and the Magic Nano-Beans* by Carl Bowen and illustrated by Omar Lozano (2015), *Goldilocks and the Three Vampires* by Laurie S. Sutton and illustrated by C. S. Jennings (2016), and *Sleeping Beauty, Magic Master* by Stephanie True Peters and illustrated by Alex Lopez (2016).

Hatke, Ben. *Zita the Spacegirl*. Illustrated by the author. First Second, 2011. Gr. 3–6.

First lines: "Finders keepers! Foosh! Hee hee! Oof! Grabbing my notebook out of my hands isn't finders keepers. Zita? This wasn't here yesterday!"

The pitch: Zita and her friend Joseph are looking at a large hole in the ground. Inside that hole is a strange gizmo. When Zita presses it, a wormhole-type thingy opens up and pulls Joseph right into it. Zita presses it again and finds herself in a weird new world with all kinds of strange aliens who look like rejects from the Star Wars movies. Zita learns that her friend Joseph has been abducted to be a human sacrifice. She sets off to save him. Zita picks up the strangest group of friends along the way, including a gigantic mouse, a hovering battle machine, a rusty robot named Randy, and a big, strong creature that answers to the name Strong-Strong.

Reading selection: Read chapter 3. Zita wakes up to a bird singing outside her window. Unknown to her, something grabs the bird and makes a "CHOMP CHOMP!" noise. Zita meets Piper, a human, and his friend Pizzicato, a giant mouse. Piper is trying hard to fix Zita's transportation device. Zita describes the creature that grabbed Joseph. Piper identifies it as a Screed. "Screed tend to wander the universe working as bounty hunters and mercenaries." Zita next finds a robot-type object, a "Heavily Armed Mobile Battle Orb," being tormented by little blue "jackanapes." Zita shoos the little fellows away and gains a new friend. The chapter ends with Zita, the giant mouse, and the battle orb in search of Joseph where, as they say, "We ride together to make our final stand."

Read-alike recommendations: The adventures of Zita continue in *Legends of Zita the Spacegirl* (2012) and *The Return of Zita the Spacegirl* (2014). The graphic novel *Target Practice*, written and illustrated by Mike Maihack (Graphix, 2014), features a heroine exploring space travel. Cleopatra's story continues in *The Thief and the Sword* (2015) and *Secret of the Time Tablets* (2016).

Jamieson, Victoria. *Roller Girl.* Illustrated by the author. Dial, 2015. Grades 4–7.

First lines: "Ugh, there's only Astrid here. I told you; only babies hang out at the park."

The pitch: That snarky comment is directed at twelve-year-old Astrid and delivered by her enemy Rachel. Her former best friend Nicole looks on in silence. Astrid tells us what led up to this incident. It began when Astrid's mother took her and Nicole to witness a Roller Derby event. Astrid became hooked. She was enthralled by the players' weird hair, tattoos, outfits, makeup, and crazy names like "Scald Eagle," "Roarshock Tess," and "Yoga Nabi Sari." Astrid's favorite player is "Rainbow Bite." To Astrid, she looks like a superhero. Astrid signed up for Junior Roller Derby Camp, designed for girls ages twelve to seventeen. She was disappointed Nicole chose Dance Camp with Rachel. Thus, the snarky comment. At one point Astrid says, "I got a very bad feeling that this summer wasn't going to go the way I planned." There's one more big problem with Astrid attending Junior Roller Derby Camp. She can't skate.

Reading selection: Read chapter 5. We follow Astrid's first day at camp. Begin where coach Heidi Go Seek says, "Hey! Do you plan on standing out here all day?" On the very first drill, the "50-Lap Killer," Astrid falls over with a "THUNK." Astrid's teammates include "Blondilocks," "Draculola," and "Slamwich." Astrid is struggling to come up with her Roller Derby name. She spends the rest of practice learning how to fall safely, performing crossovers, and executing the pushcart drill. End the reading where Astrid says, "WAAAAHH!" Add an extra comment pointing out that author Victoria Jamieson is a Roller Derby skater in real life and she goes by the name Winnie the Pow.

Read-alike recommendations: The series Dorothy's Derby Chronicles by Meghan Dougherty features Roller Derby girls in a chapter book format. The two titles are *Rise of the Undead Redhead* (Sourcebooks Jabberwocky, 2014) and *Woe of Jade Doe* (2015).

Lucke, Deb. *The Lunch Witch*. Illustrated by the author. Papercutz, 2015. Gr. 4–7.

First line: "For generations and generations, the women of my family have stirred up trouble in a big, black pot."

The pitch: Grunhilda thinks she'll be able to support herself selling her family's potions. After all, her "great-great-great-great-great-great-great-great-great-grandmother invented the recipe for Hansel-and-Gretel pie" and her great-great-great-great-great-great-aunt Tituba created the "Most Foul Porridge," made up of the souls of thirteen cats. The trouble is that "nobody really believes in magic anymore" and Grunhilda has to search for a job. She failed at being a fake witch for the Salem Haunted Museum. She wasn't scary enough. Grunhilda is discouraged. "There're not a lot of employment opportunities for someone who can make milk curdle just by breathing." She finally gets a job as an elementary school lunch lady but is almost immediately blackmailed by a girl named Madison. They strike a deal. Madison wants a potion to make her smart. Madison says, "I can give you 75¢. Oh . . . I only have 37¢."

Reading selection: Read the second half of chapter 9, where Grunhilda looks at her recipe and says, "Finally, I can—huh?" In order to make the Intelligence Potion, Grunhilda needs black gall, school paste, Thousand Island dressing, an earwig, and the nose hair of a principal. Through a series of close-up maneuvers, she manages to pluck that nose hair with tweezers. Continue reading into chapter 10. Grunhilda and Madison finalize the deal. Grunhilda tells the girl to "take a dab of this, rub it on your forehead and Poof! You're a genius." The potion backfires and Madison turns into a frog. As she's transforming, Madison is confused. "Do smart kids have long tongues? Long tongues that unfurl from the front of their mouths? What is happening to me? Is it puberty?" End the selection where Grunhilda asks, "Who's there? Hey, isn't that Madison's backpack? How . . . Oy!"

Read-alike recommendations: The sequel is titled *Knee-Deep in Niceness* (2016). *Baba Yaga's Assistant* by Marika McCoola (Candlewick, 2015) is a graphic novel about a girl named Masha who applies for the job to clean and cook for a notorious witch.

McCranie, Stephen. *The Biggest, Bestest Time Ever!* (Mal and Chad series). Illustrated by the author. Philomel, 2011. Gr. 3–5.

First line: "What are you making?"

The pitch: Fourth grader Mal is telling his talking dog Chad (that's right, a talking dog) that he is making a jet pack backpack (that's right, a jet pack backpack). Mal says, "Instead of riding the bus to school, I'm going to start flying to school." Unfortunately, the jet pack backpack fails the safety test and makes a hole in Mal's roof. He covers the hole with a poster. Mal's teacher gives the class an essay homework assignment: What do you want to be when you grow up? Mal doesn't know. He creates a "mini-mega-morpher" from his mother's vacuum cleaner. It might help him decide if he wants to be a scuba diver. After he shrinks both himself and Chad, the two climb into the kitchen sink full of dirty dishes. Chad asks, "Are you ready for the biggest, bestest time you ever had?" Mal replies, "Is bestest a word? I don't think bestest is a word."

Reading selection: Read the last section of chapter 2, "Don't Be Such a Cry-Puppy," when Chad asks, "So now do you know what you want to be when you grow up?" Mal's mother comes home. She sees both the vacuum cleaner and the dirty sink and gets angry. Mal and Chad change back to normal size. Mom asks, "Did you rig the vacuum cleaner as some kind of prank, Mal?" She sends Mal and Chad to bed without dinner. End the passage where Mom yells, "Mal! Why did you put a poster on your ceiling?"

Read-alike recommendations: The sequels are *Food Fight!* (2012) and *Belly Flop!* (2012). The graphic novel *Copper*, written and illustrated by Kazu Kibuishi (Graphix, 2010), features the silly adventures of a boy and his dog.

Rex, Michael. *Fangbone! Third-Grade Barbarian*. Illustrated by the author. Putnam, 2012. Gr. 3–4.

First line: "In a world of swords, magic, barbarians, and evil big toes . . . Fangbone!"

The pitch: Warriors are ordering the undersized but brave Fangbone to sharpen their swords, fix their shields, and pick the spider eggs from their armpits. Fangbone refuses. "Pick your own armpits, you swamp-water grease-fish!"

He declares that he is a warrior, but the adults only laugh and insult him back. "You are lower to the ground than a pus-filled pimple on the belly of a slop-hog!" During a battle, Fangbone is charged with taking something called "The Big Toe of Drool" to a sorcerer who sends him to . . . our world.

Reading selection: Start on page 20. Fangbone lands in a town dump and proceeds to attack a rusty old truck. He spots an elementary school and tries to blend in with the students. He befriends a hyperactive boy named Bill. The other students ask if Fangbone is his first or last name. He replies, "I am Fangbone the Young, of the Mighty Lizard Clan. Son of Steelbeard the Bold, Grandson to Lockjaw the Fearless. Great-grandson of Weasel-Eye the Slippery!" The kids pester him with more questions. "Why do you wear that helmet? Why is your underwear made out of fur? Do you like glitter?" The final question is: "Why did you come to our school?" Fangbone gives a passionate speech about protecting the Big Toe of Drool and the story of the evil Drool who was defeated and cut into pieces. At this point the teacher says, "WHOA! Fangbone, this might not be appropriate for our classroom." Of course, the kids clamor for more. Over the years, Drool has been reassembling himself, missing only his big toe. If he is reunited with this appendage, he will rule once more. End the passage right after Fangbone pronounces he is the protector of the toe and the teacher says, "Uh . . . Fangbone, we don't stand on desks. Please take a seat."

Read-alike recommendations: Fangbone's quest continues with *The Egg of Misery* (2012) and *The Birthday Party of Dread* (2012). The graphic novel *The Adventures of Ook and Gluk: Kung-Fu Cavemen from the Future*, written and illustrated by Dav Pilkey (Blue Sky, 2010), features two young heroes who go back and forth in time to save the day.

Stine, R. L. *Creepy Creatures* (Goosebumps Graphix series). Illustrated by Gabriel Hernandez, Greg Ruth, and Scott Morse. Scholastic, 2006. Gr. 4–7.
First line: "It all began when we moved to Florida."
The pitch: To be precise, that's moving-to-Florida-right-next-to-a-scary-swamp-with-a-werewolf-in-it. That's the first story in this horror collection. The second story features walking scarecrows. These two tales are guaranteed to keep readers awake at night. More like stay-awake-with-the-lights-on-at-night kind of awake. If that's not enough, read the third story about a father who takes his kids to Alaska to take pictures of the Abominable Snowman. The locals said it was seen eating human bones. If these stories sound somewhat familiar, they are all from R. L. Stine's famous Goosebumps series and turned into comic book style. Back to the werewolf story. Grady and his sister Emily have moved to the edge of a swamp with their scientist parents, who are studying swamp deer.
Reading selection: Begin on the fourth page where Emily says, "Yuck. Gnats. I hate gnats." The two kids are exploring the swamp when they come upon a hut in the middle of the swamp. The door opens with a "CCCRREEEAAAKKKK."

A scary man, known as the Swamp Hermit, peeks out and the kids run scream-ing. Grady meets a neighbor kid named Will who shares the origin of Fever Swamp. Later, Grady wakes up to the sound of howling. Something is scratching at the front door. End the reading when Grady opens the door the next morning and a large dog or wolf jumps on him. Grady says, "WHOOAAAAA!!"

Read-alike recommendations: There are three graphic novel versions of the Goosebumps series. The other two titles are *Terror Trips* (2007) and *Scary Summer* (2007). Another volume, *Slappy's Tales of Horror* (2015), revisits some of the graphic novel story versions.

Telgemeier, Raina. *Smile*. Scholastic, 2010. Gr. 4–7.

First line: "Smile!!"

The pitch: That's one of the last times sixth grader Raina smiles with a full set of teeth for quite some time. Right after attending a Scout meeting, Raina trips and falls on her face. She checks herself and thinks, "Hands . . . legs . . . nothing broken. Cool." Then she sees blood. Raina is rushed to the dentist because her front teeth have been knocked out. Actually, one tooth was knocked out and the other was pushed up into her gums. When she wakes up the next morning and checks the mirror, she asks, "What'th thith thtuff on my teeth??" On a return trip, the dentist removes the white plaster seal covering her teeth and says, "Uh-oh."

Reading selection: Start reading page 24 where the dentist says, "When you knocked them out, you must have damaged the bone above, too." Raina thinks she looks like a vampire because her front teeth are set higher up than the rest of them. Her Scout troop reacts with comments like, "Um, you don't look *that* weird" and "It's . . . not as bad as . . . before." Raina learns she'll have to wear headgear. "But . . . but I'm gonna look like a nerd with headgear on," she com-plains to the dentist, who assures her that it's only for wearing at night. After her ears are pierced and she has even more procedures done to her teeth, Raina com-plains to her father that "My whole head hurts so much." End the reading on page 45 where her father tells her to bang her head on the wall. "That way, when you stop banging, it'll hurt less." Raina says, "Thanks for the sympathy, Dad."

Read-alike recommendations: Raina has another autobiographical graphic novel about her childhood with *Sisters* (2014). *El Deafo*, written and illustrated by Cece Bell (Abrams, 2015), is the autobiographical graphic novel about a girl who lost her hearing due to spinal meningitis.

Winick, Judd. *The Boy Who Crashed to Earth* (Hilo series). Random House, 2015. Gr. 4–6.

First line: "AAAAAH!"

The pitch: "AAAAAH" is the sound D.J. and his new friend make on the day they meet. D.J. is having another ordinary, boring day in his ordinary, boring life when he sees a ball of energy fall from the sky. It makes a small crater in the ground. Lying inside the crater is a boy dressed only in silver shorts. When D.J. reaches out to the boy, he is shocked backward, as if a lightning bolt struck him. The boy does not remember who he is. D.J. takes him home and the strange kid slowly remembers his name. "High-Low. My name is Hilo." He also remembers that they are in danger from something called Razorwark.

Reading selection: Read chapter 5, "Nothing New Ever Happens Here." Something else falls from the sky and crashes into the ground. D.J., his best friend Gina, and Hilo find the new crater. They are attacked by a "robot ant," a Rant. As the Rant is about to crush D.J., Hilo unleashes laser bolts from his hands, knocking out the Rant. It recovers and chases the trio once again. D.J. pushes the Rant over a cliff. Stop the passage where Gina asks if Hilo is okay and D.J. responds, "Not exactly."

Read-alike recommendations: The other titles in the Hilo trilogy include *Saving the Whole Wide World* (2016) and *The Great Big Boom* (2017). *Earthling*, written and illustrated by Mark Fearing (Chronicle, 2012), is a science fiction graphic novel that features Bud, who accidentally gets on the wrong school bus and winds up at a school in outer space.

CHAPTER 3

Fantasy

Ever since the publication of the first Harry Potter book in 1998, fantasy has replaced contemporary realistic fiction as the most popular genre with young readers. Fantasy is characterized mostly by the presence of magic in the story. Sometimes the magic is subtle and sometimes it is the key focus of the book.

Anderson, Jodi Lynn. *My Diary from the Edge of the World.* **Aladdin, 2015. Gr. 4–7.**

First lines: "I'm on top of the hill, looking down on the town of Cliffden, Maine. It's an early fall day, and so far no one's noticed that I'm not where I'm supposed to be."

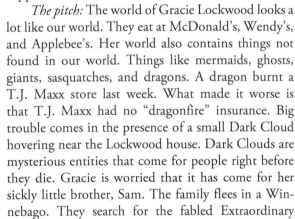

The pitch: The world of Gracie Lockwood looks a lot like our world. They eat at McDonald's, Wendy's, and Applebee's. Her world also contains things not found in our world. Things like mermaids, ghosts, giants, sasquatches, and dragons. A dragon burnt a T.J. Maxx store last week. What made it worse is that T.J. Maxx had no "dragonfire" insurance. Big trouble comes in the presence of a small Dark Cloud hovering near the Lockwood house. Dark Clouds are mysterious entities that come for people right before they die. Gracie is worried that it has come for her sickly little brother, Sam. The family flees in a Winnebago. They search for the fabled Extraordinary World where Dark Clouds don't exist. On the way, they stop in the dark woods where Gracie's grandmother, a scary witch, lives.

Reading selection: Read Gracie's entry for "October 21st." Gracie writes, "I am in a sleeping bag in the woods, in the ghost-infested, witch-infested, sasquatch-infested Smoky Mountains." A warning sign near the trailhead reads: "HIKING AND CAMPING MAY RESULT IN DISMEMBERMENT BY SASQUATCH, WITCH, OR BEAR, AND POSSIBLE KIDNAPPING BY SPECTRAL INHABITANTS. PLEASE RESPECT DESIGNATED WILD-LIFE AND WITCHCRAFT AREAS." Gracie reports that their first day of hiking wasn't too bad. They saw a few tree demons and a witch village behind a locked gate, but actually she and her sister Millie are bored. The chapter ends with Gracie finding some raccoon poo. She says, "I'm planning to put it in one of Millie's hiking boots once she falls asleep."

Read-alike recommendations: Author Anderson has also written the May Bird series featuring a girl who lives near woods where people have vanished. The titles in the trilogy are *May Bird and the Ever After* (2006), *May Bird among the Stars* (2007), and *May Bird: Warrior Princess* (2008).

Durst, Sarah Beth. *The Girl Who Could Not Dream.* **Clarion, 2015. Gr. 4–6.**

First line: "Sophie had only ever stolen one dream."

The pitch: Sophie's parents own the Dreamcatcher Bookstore and, in the basement, is their other store. Their secret store. The Dream Shop. The shop sells all types of dreams. "There were beach dreams and outer-space dreams and falling-through-empty-air dreams, lost-loved-ones dreams and first-love-dreams, ordinary-life dreams and late-for-the-bus dreams, and of course, monster dreams." Sophie grabs an unlabeled bottle and drinks the contents. "She plunged instantly into the dream." It turns out to be a "monster-in-the-closet" dream. The monster tries to scare Sophie with its "three rows of shiny, sharp, shark-like teeth," but Sophie surprisingly compliments it. She says, "You have beautiful iri-descent fur. That means you shine with different colors. You're a very handsome monster." The two become close friends. When Sophie wakes up, the monster joins her in the real world. Sophie assures her parents the monster is friendly. Sophie's mother warns the monster, "If you mean my daughter any harm, I will personally skin you before shoving you back into a dream." The monster prom-ises to be good. "And that was how Monster came to join Sophie's family." One day, Monster joins Sophie at her school.

Reading selection: Read the beginning of chapter 8. Monster warns Sophie not to go out into the school hallway. She does anyway and follows Monster into the music room where a strange "lanky, translucent-gray creature that looked like a cross between a giraffe and a man—if a giraffe had razor-like claws instead of hooves" is attacking a boy named Ethan. Monster drives the creature away. Sophie and Monster try to convince Ethan it's all a bad dream. Monster starts singing, "Do-do, do-do, do-do. Ripple, ripple, ripple" and explains he is "mak-ing that dream-sequence sound they do on TV." End the selection where Ethan says, "Let's go."

Read-alike recommendation: Finding Serendipity by Angelica Banks (Holt, 2015) is a fantasy about a girl who goes searching for her missing mother in a land of stories.

Goebel, Jenny. *Fortune Falls.* Scholastic, 2016. Gr. 4–6.

First line: "Petey's sweaty little hand wriggled in mine."

The pitch: Petey is Sadie's little brother. She is pointing out Tommy's mother to Petey, and that is enough to make her sibling settle down. Tommy's mother is wearing a halo cast because her back was broken. You know that saying: "Step on a crack, break your mother's back"? That's what happened to Tommy's mom. Petey, Sadie, and their neighbors live in Fortune Falls, a town where superstitions, both good and bad, are real. Folks don't try to leave Fortune Falls. They're likely to have a heart attack trying to escape. Some kids who live in Fortune Falls are the lucky kids. Good things always happen to them. They can apparently do no wrong. And then, there are the Unluckys. They constantly have bad luck. Like the girl who broke a mirror. Within the hour, she died. Another girl broke a mirror and "her entire family had been sucked into a sinkhole." And Sadie? Let's just say she's a "vacuum for bad luck, a magnet for misfortune."

Reading selection: Read the last half of chapter 5, "Seven Years Bad Luck," beginning with the sentence: "The tree house, tucked as it was among the maple leaves and cut off from everything else, had been one of the few places—much like my bedroom—where I truly felt happy and safe." Sadie's friend Cooper gives her an early birthday present. It's a telescope to help the unlucky Sadie see a star and make a wish. When she goes to hug Cooper, the telescope falls. When Cooper inspects the telescope, he gasps and says, "'Sadie, there was a mirror inside . . . probably to reflect the light . . . and . . .' He was still stalling, but I knew. 'It's broken.'"

Read-alike recommendation: Just My Luck by Cammie McGovern (Harper, 2016) is a modern realistic book about a boy named Benny who is going through a streak of bad luck. He's even convinced that he's the reason his father had to go to the hospital.

Laybourn, Emma. *Missing Magic.* Dial, 2007. Gr. 4–6.

First line: "The teacher was watching me, all the time."

The pitch: Imagine a kid enrolled at a school like Hogwarts in the Harry Potter series who can't perform any magic. That's similar to what happens to eleven-year-old Ned when he tries to pass a simple magic test. His parents have magical powers, his little sisters have magical powers, and everyone else who lives in Leodwych City has magical powers. Except Ned. He is what they call "magically challenged." Ned doesn't pass the test of stacking wooden blocks with magic but he gets into Leodwych School anyway, a school that is "ancient and famous, steeped in magic." His Uncle Kelver is one of the most famous magical beings in the land and pays for Ned's tuition. Immediately, Ned becomes the focus of school pranks. His bedsheets tie themselves around him, his pencils levitate, and his hair turns into snakes. Ned wonders, "How long was it going to be like this? Was I going to be tricked and tripped every step of the way? I had to learn magic and fast. Until then, I had nothing to fight back with. Nothing at all."

Reading selection: Read the first part of chapter 4. Ned is looking forward to magic lessons. Perhaps he can develop some powers. He has trouble with the desk lid that snaps like a crocodile and the chair that turns into jelly. He grabs another chair, but it floats high above the class with Ned on it. Their teacher, Mr. Wragg, comes in and tells the class, "Open your copies of *First Mage* to chapter two." The kids want to talk about the horror stalking the land, Necromancers who kidnap children. Wragg demands the children return to their studies. Ned interrupts with another question about the Necromancers, causing Wragg to ask, "Are you being impertinent, boy?" End the reading where Wragg yells, "'No more questions!' He was working himself into a fine old froth. So I decided to shelve my questions for now, got out my rare and expensive pencils, and began to write."

Read-alike recommendations: Remarkable by Lizzie K. Foley (Dial, 2012) is the story of an ordinary girl who lives in a place where everyone else is an overachiever. *The Power of Poppy Pendle* by Natasha Lowe (Paula Wiseman, 2012) is a fantasy about a girl who is born to ordinary parents but who herself has witch magic powers. Its companion books include *The Courage of Cat Campbell* (2015) and *The Marvelous Magic of Miss Mable* (2016).

Mlynowski, Sarah. *Fairest of All* (Whatever After series). Scholastic, 2012. Gr. 4–6.

First lines: "Once upon a time my life was normal. Then the mirror in our basement ate us."

The pitch: Jonah leads his ten-year-old sister Abby to the basement of their new home to check out a mirror the previous owners had left behind. "The frame is made of stone and decorated with carvings of small fairies with wings and wands. I don't know why the old owners didn't take it with them, except . . . well, it's creepy." Jonah knocks on the mirror and it starts hissing. He knocks a second time and a purple light radiates from the mirror. He knocks a third time and the siblings are sucked into the mirror. They find themselves deep in a forest. They spot an old woman wearing a black coat and carrying a basket of apples.

Reading selection: Read the very end of chapter 5, "Hide and Seek," beginning with the line: "We follow the old lady for another five minutes, until we arrive at a house." The kids see the old lady knock on the door. The chapter ends with the sentence: "And finally, the curtain behind one of the windows twitches." Continue reading chapter 6, "An Apple a Day." They see a young woman with dark hair and pale skin. "Super pale, except *not* in a zombie way.

More like in a china doll way. And her lips are really red. Really, really red. Like, bloodred, but again, not in a *bad* bloodred way. She's beautiful, actually. Also, she looks familiar, like I've seen her before." Jonah runs up to the old lady and asks for one of her apples. Abby and Jonah make the old lady mad, and she leaves with a "terrifying high-pitched laugh." End the passage where Jonah shivers and says, "I think I want to go home now."

Read-alike recommendations: This is the first book in the Whatever After series. The other titles include *If the Shoe Fits* (2013), *Sink or Swim* (2013), *Dream On* (2013), *Bad Hair Day* (2014), *Cold as Ice* (2014), *Beauty Queen* (2015), *Once upon a Frog* (2015), *Genie in a Bottle* (2016), and *Sugar and Spice* (2016).

Mlynowski, Sarah, Lauren Myracle, and Emily Jenkins. *Upside Down Magic.* **Scholastic, 2015. Gr. 4–6.**

First line: "Nory Horace was trying to turn herself into a kitten."

The pitch: Elinor, or Nory as she's called, was hoping that this time she wouldn't turn into a puppy-squid or a skunk-elephant. She has turned into those animal combinations before. Her test is to turn into a normal-looking little kitten. If Nory passes, she will be able to join her brother and sister at the Sage Academy, where her father is the headmaster. If she doesn't pass the test, she might have to go to a special class in another school, a class called Upside Down Magic, for kids who can't control their magical abilities. Things aren't looking good for Nory as she practices. She turns into a beaver-kitten, a "bitten," and the beaver part of her takes over her girl mind. The bitten chews the furniture and books in her father's study. Poor Nory's magic is "wonky."

Reading selection: Read chapter 4. Nory is in the Hall of Magic and Performance, standing in front of four teachers and her father. She is ordered to turn herself into a black kitten. Things start well but then she becomes a "mitten," a snake-kitten. The mitten bites her father's hand and quickly turns into a dragon-kitten. When Nory finally turns herself back into a girl, she thanks the committee. The teachers are busy writing in their notebooks and her father is "cradling his swelling hand. His swelling, bleeding hand." The chapter ends with Nory's father telling her, "Elinor Boxwood Horace, your admission is denied."

Read-alike recommendations: The sequels are *Sticks and Stones* (2016) and *Showing Off* (2016). *Ordinary Magic* by Caitlen Rubino-Bradway (Bloomsbury, 2012) features a world where everyone is magical except Abbey. She is sent to a boarding school to help her deal with her unmagical disability.

Reeve, Philip. *Oliver and the Sea Monkeys* **(A Not-So-Impossible Tale series). Random House, 2014. Gr. 3–5. Previously published as** *Oliver and the Seawigs.*

First line: "Oliver Crisp was only ten years old, but they had been a busy and exciting ten years, because Oliver's mother and father were explorers."

The pitch: Oliver's parents disappeared when they went exploring strange islands. The islands are actually living creatures called the Rambling Isles. Kind of like big stony giants. The visible island part is their head and the grass is their hair. These giants like to decorate their tops with wigs made up of things they find in the sea. Oliver learns his parents have been kidnapped by one particularly mean Rambling Isle named the Thurlstone, who is accompanied by a cruel human kid named Stacey. Oliver goes after his missing parents and is joined by new friends, including a mouthy albatross named Mr. Culpepper and a nearsighted mermaid named Iris. Some very sarcastic seaweed follows them to see what happens. Sarcastic seaweed. Rambling Isles. It will eventually all make sense. . . .

Reading selection: Read the second half of chapter 5, beginning with the sentence: "Oliver just cupped his hands around his mouth and shouted, 'Give me back my mom and dad!'" Oliver is shouting at Stacey de Lacey who is mad because he has a girl's name. Stacey insists that his name "is one of those names that can be for a boy or a girl! Like Hilary or Leslie, or . . . um." Stop after the long sentence: "From the giant statues that grinned and snarled came a rumbling, a whispering, a scrabbling, a jostling, a strange, demented jabbering. . . ." Pick up the reading with the line: "That's what the green tide was, pouring out of the mouths and eyes of the Thurlstone's old stone heads and rushing across the sea." The tide is Stacey's army of sea monkeys with their green fur. After Stacey and the Thurlstone repel Oliver and his friends and make off with Oliver's parents, the chapter ends with the sarcastic seaweed stating, "That went well!"

Read-alike recommendations: The other books in the series are *Cakes in Space* (2016), the story of a girl who makes cakes that come alive and try to destroy her spaceship, and *Pugs of the Frozen North* (2016), about two kids who run a dogsled with sixty-six pugs.

Riordan, Rick. *The Lost Hero* (Heroes of Olympus series). Hyperion, 2010. Gr. 5–7.

First line: "Even before he got electrocuted, Jason was having a rotten day."

The pitch: Jason wakes up in the backseat of a school bus, holding the hand of a girl he doesn't know. He has truly lost his memory. He is told the bus is heading to Wilderness School, an institution for kids with behavior problems. Jason protests he's not supposed to be there. Leo, the boy sitting in front of Jason, laughs and says, "Yeah, right, Jason. We've all been framed! I didn't run away six times. Piper didn't steal a BMW." Piper is the girl holding hands with Jason. Up until today, Leo has never seen anything wilder than a "rattlesnake in the cow pasture and his Aunt Rosa in her nightgown." These three kids turn out to be demigods or "half-bloods." One of their parents is a Greek/Roman god or goddess. When the bus stops at the Grand Canyon for a visit, we learn another student, Dylan, isn't really a student at all.

Reading selection: Read a portion of chapter 2, beginning with the paragraph: "Dylan's body dissolved into smoke, as if his molecules were coming unglued. He had the same face, the same brilliant white smile, but his whole form was suddenly composed of swirling black vapor, his eyes like electrical sparks in a living storm cloud. He sprouted black smoky wings and rose above the skywalk." Dylan is a "ventus," a storm spirit. He is joined by two more storm spirits. Dylan hurls a blast of electricity at Jason's chest. "The lightning bolt had gone straight through his body and blasted off his left shoe." Jason gets back up and dispatches the two other storm spirits. End the passage where Dylan cries out, "Impossible! Who *are* you, half-blood?"

Read-alike recommendations: The stories of Jason, Piper, and Leo continue in *The Son of Neptune* (2011), *The Mark of Athena* (2012), *The House of Hades* (2013), and *The Blood of Olympus* (2014). This series is an offshoot of the popular Percy Jackson and the Olympians series that includes *The Lightning Thief* (2005), *The Sea of Monsters* (2006), *The Titan's Curse* (2007), *The Battle of the Labyrinth* (2008), and *The Last Olympian* (2009). For graphic novel fans, *The Lost Hero* appears in this format, written by Rick Riordan and Robert Venditti and illustrated by Nate Powell (2014).

Selfors, Suzanne. *The Sasquatch Escape* (Imaginary Veterinary series). Little, Brown, 2013. Gr. 3–5.

First line: "The weird shadow swept across the sky."

The pitch: Ten-year-old Ben swears he sees something "moving between the clouds—something with an enormous wingspan and a long tail." Ben is spending the summer with his Grandpa Abe in Buttonville, a town striving to survive ever since the old button factory went out of business. Ben sees the shadowy sight again in town. He is positive a local girl, Pearl, has also seen it. He spots her mouthing the word "dragon." Ben learns that a Dr. Woo is renting the button factory. Back at home, Grandpa Abe's cat Barnaby drops something from its mouth in Ben's bedroom. "The creature's body and wings were black, but one of the wings was torn. Was it a bat?" The tiny creature has scales and breathes fire. Ben and Pearl take their discovery, a tiny dragon, to the button factory. While there, a sasquatch escapes. Since it was partly Ben's fault, the kids are given instructions on how to capture the sasquatch.

Reading selection: Read chapter 12. Pearl and Ben are looking through *Dr. Woo's Guide to Catching a Sasquatch.* There are very specific instructions. The first is that "this book will not help you catch any other two-legged creature, such as a yeti or a troll or a leprechaun." One has to refer to Dr. Woo's other instruction books to catch those. The second is that while the sasquatch looks stupid, it is anything but. "It enjoys puzzles and likes to arrange things by color." The manual goes on to state that the sasquatch is over four hundred pounds, has a strong odor, hates being asked too many questions, is always hungry, and while mostly gentle, will tear off your limbs if you make it angry. Further directions describe how to use a tranquilizer dart to put it to sleep. "If you are unable to carry a sasquatch, do not use the tranquilizer dart." A special whistle should only be used as a last resort because it might "attract creatures other than the sasquatch." As the chapter ends, Pearl puts the whistle to her lips and blows it.

Read-alike recommendations: There are several more titles in the series, including *The Lonely Lake Monster* (2013), *The Rain Dragon Rescue* (2014), *The Order of the Unicorn* (2014), *The Griffin's Riddle* (2015), and *The Fairy Swarm* (2015).

Sutherland, Tui T., and Kari Sutherland. *The Menagerie*. Harper, 2013. Gr. 5–7.

First line: "Logan Wilde noticed the feathers as soon as he woke up."

The pitch: One of the feathers is huge and glows in the sunlight. Logan's cat is hiding in the closet, his mice are huddled under their wood shavings, the Siamese fighting fish is swimming frantically, and the goldfish bowl is empty. When Logan heads off to school, "it never occurred to him that his nighttime visitor might not have left." At school, something has eaten all the cafeteria food. Three kids—Blue, Zoe, and Keiko—are talking strangely about a missing . . . dog. Something weird is going on. When Logan gets back home, he finds out.

Reading selection: Read the very end of chapter 2 with the sentence: "With a shrug, Logan went into his room, dropped his backpack, and checked on the mouse cage." His mice are still frightened, and Logan notices their food canister is empty. Just then, a loud "SQUUUUUUUUUUUOOOOOOOOOOOOOOORP" erupts from somewhere. Logan sees a long golden tail. The chapter ends with the line: "There was a monster under his bed." Continue reading the beginning of chapter 3. Logan grabs his baseball bat as he inspects the creature. "The front half of it looked like a giant golden eagle, wings and beak and all. The rest of its body was furry, with sharp lion claws on its four paws." The creature opens its eyes and Logan hears in his head: "Looooooooogan!" Logan realizes that he is looking at something that is supposed to be mythical, a gryphon. Instead of attacking Logan, the gryphon jumps into his lap. End the selection with the words: "Its dark eyes stared at him earnestly, and when it head-butted his chest, he couldn't resist reaching out to pat it."

Read-alike recommendations: The other two titles in the trilogy featuring Logan, Zoe, and the mythical creatures are *Dragon on Trial* (2014) and

Krakens and Lies (2015). *Fablehaven* by Brandon Mull (Simon & Schuster, 2007) is the first title in a series about two kids who learn their grandfather is the caretaker of a magical place filled with mythical creatures. The sequels are *Rise of the Evening Star* (2007), *Grip of the Shadow Plague* (2009), *Secrets of the Dragon Sanctuary* (2010), and *Keys to the Demon Prison* (2011). *Pip Bartlett's Guide to Magical Creatures* by Jackson Pearce and Maggie Stiefvater (Scholastic, 2016) is the story of a girl who can communicate with magical creatures when no one else can.

Yep, Laurence, and Joanne Ryder. *A Dragon's Guide to the Care and Feeding of Humans*. Crown, 2015. Gr. 4–7.

First line: "It was a lovely funeral for Fluffy, the best pet I ever had."

The pitch: The narrator of that line is a dragon and its pet Fluffy was a human, a very old lady known to her relatives as Great-Aunt Amelia. Her niece Winnie barges into the dragon's underground lair and learns that its name is Miss Drake. Winnie thinks that Miss Drake should be her pet. The three-thousand-year-old dragon Miss Drake is used to running things, but ten-year-old Winnie is just as headstrong. The two learn to stop butting heads and work together because Winnie, unfortunately, has unleashed some dangerous magic upon the world.

Reading selection: Read chapter 6. Winnie shows up at Miss Drake's home intending to show the dragon the drawings she did in her new sketchbook. When they discover the drawings are gone, Miss Drake has an uneasy feeling that there was magic in the book. Trying to calm down, Miss Drake asks Winnie how many drawings she created. "Winnie took a sip. 'Umpteen.' I told myself to be patient. 'Umpteen is not as precise a figure as I would like.'" They figure out that Winnie drew twenty creatures and that those images came to life. The chapter ends with the two setting off to retrieve these creatures and magically return them back into the sketchbook. Miss Drake tries to sniff out the first creature. "'It must be so small that I can't find its scent,' I said. I trusted my snout more than I did my eyes, so I dismissed my suspicions—and made things even worse."

Read-alike recommendations: *How to Train Your Dragon* by Cressida Cowell (Little, Brown, 2004) follows young Hiccup as he tries to pass his tribe's initiation test by capturing and training a live dragon. The books in this series are *How to Be a Pirate* (2004), *How to Speak Dragonese* (2005), *How to Cheat a Dragon's Curse* (2006), *How to Twist a Dragon's Tale* (2008), *A Hero's Guide to Deadly Dragons* (2009), *How to Ride a Dragon's Storm* (2010), *How to Break a Dragon's Heart* (2011), *How to Steal a Dragon's Sword* (2012), *How to Seize a Dragon's Jewel* (2013), *How to Betray a Dragon's Hero* (2013), and *How to Fight a Dragon's Fury* (2015).

CHAPTER 4

Horror

Horror fiction is a subcategory of both fantasy, where magic is present and responsible for characters like witches and ghosts, and also science fiction, where science is the result of the horror characters, like Frankenstein's monster and zombies. While sharing horror with young readers might bother some adults, it might just be the type of genre for the right reluctant reader. Some kids love those scary, vicarious thrills.

Berry, Julie Gardner, and Sally Faye Gardner. *The Rat Brain Fiasco* **(Splurch Academy for Disruptive Boys series). Grosset & Dunlap, 2010. Gr. 3–6.**

First line: "A Word of Warning to All Disruptive Boys: The story you are about to read is true."

The pitch: It's true that Cody has earned two binders full of reports of bad behavior at the Splurch Academy for Disruptive Boys, but Cody sees it otherwise. "'I haven't been that bad lately, have I?' he thought. 'Well, there was that

rotten egg thing. Big deal. And then there was the fire. Yep, come to think of it, definitely the fire.'" It's also true that Cody's regular school and his parents signed off to send him to Splurch Academy where the strange-looking Dr. Farley specializes in working with naughty kids. And it is so, so true that Cody bolts from his new boarding school not long after his arrival, straight down a trapdoor.

Reading selection: Read chapter 5, "The Dungeon." Cody first notices the pain. "Then, the dark. Then, the *squeaks*." Cody finds himself covered in a river of rats. He climbs up onto the low-hanging slimy pipes and heads for a window. "A huge spider—probably a tarantula—crawled across his hands. Rats ran along the pipes like tightrope walkers. Centipedes reared up and waved fifty or sixty legs at him." Cody makes it to the window, but it won't open. Perhaps just as well because he sees the shadows of things flying and slithering outside. The chapter ends with the lines: "Farley *wasn't* bluffing when he said there were ferocious beasts around here. Or maybe Cody's eyes were just playing spooky tricks on him, because it was late and he was tired and hungry and far away from home."

Read-alike recommendations: Cody and the other disruptive boys are enrolled in Splurch Academy for three more books: *Curse of the Bizarro Beetle* (2010), *The Colossal Fossil Freakout* (2011), and *The Trouble with Squids* (2011). *Dr. Critchlore's School for Minions* by Sheila Grau (Amulet, 2015) is the story of a school where the students and teachers are monsters. Its sequel is *Gorilla Tactics* (2016).

Cooper, Rose. *I Text Dead People.* **Delacorte, 2015. Gr. 5–7.**

First line: "There's no such things as ghosts."

The pitch: That's what thirteen-year-old Annabel Craven tells herself as she walks among the tombstones that border her new house. She tries to reassure herself that "dead people stay dead." On the first day to her new school, she trips, falls, and hears a male voice say, "Don't move." The voice belongs to a tall teen who tells her that she has something that belongs to him. Annabel escapes by running into a forest. There, she finds a cell phone and receives the following text message on the phone: "Help me." Annabel tries to delete the message but it remains. The phone buzzes with a new text: "I said I need help. Why won't you help me?"

Reading selection: Read chapter 12. Annabel leaves a party and gets another strange text. This time the sender identifies herself as Jane Doe whose grave is the only one without flowers. "And I'm wedged in between Margaret Meyers and Dorothy Quinn, two horrible old snoots I can't get away from." Annabel believes that one of her classmates, Millie, is playing a prank. She heads to a park to meet up with Millie. Annabel is all alone when she hears strange noises. "There were two sagging swings. One of them began to stir." She feels a hand on her shoulder and sees a little boy. His name is Tommy and he's four. When Annabel asks Tommy where he lives, the boy points to the ground by her feet. He then vanishes right in front of her. Annabel thinks she is hallucinating and waits for the boy to return. The chapter ends with the sentence: "When it didn't, she took off at a run, catching the smell of chocolate and the distant laughter of a little boy."

Read-alike recommendation: Texting the Underworld by Ellen Booraem (Dial, 2013) is the story of Conor, a modern-day boy who communicates with Ashling, a banshee spirit.

Donbavand, Tommy. *Fang of the Vampire* **(Scream Street series). Candlewick, 2009. Gr. 3–6.**

First line: "The schoolboy leaped over the wall into the graveyard, his feet skidding on the wet grass."

The pitch: The poor schoolboy is being pursued by a werewolf. The werewolf, a kid named Luke, is actually teaching the schoolboy, a bully, a lesson. Luke's parents, both normal people, are worried about him. "Neither of his parents had smiled for a long time. Not since he had first transformed into a werewolf." Luke and his parents are captured by agents of G.H.O.U.L., the Government Housing of Unusual Lifeforms. They are sent to live on Scream Street. Their new neighbors, the Negative family—Alston, Bella, and their son Resus—are vampires.

Reading selection: Read the last paragraph of chapter 3, "The Attack," beginning with the line: "The vampire climbed out of the bush and ran on." Something grabs Luke's ankle. The chapter ends with the words: "It was a zombie." Continue reading chapter 4, "The Transformation." The zombie grins at Luke, "revealing a mouth crawling with worms and maggots. A cockroach scuttled out of a nostril and up into the zombie's left ear, dragging a trail of black snot behind it." The zombie surprises Luke by saying, "Dude! What's the scoop?" End the reading with the line: "As Resus helped him to his feet, Luke made a mental note to be much kinder to computer-game zombies from now on."

Read-alike recommendations: There are twelve more books in the series: *Blood of the Witch* (2009), *Heart of the Mummy* (2009), *Flesh of the Zombie* (2009), *Skull of the Skeleton* (2009), *Claw of the Werewolf* (2009), *Invasion of the Normals* (2009), *Attack of the Trolls* (2010), *Terror of the Nightwatchman* (2010), *Rampage of the Goblins* (2015), *Hunger of the Yetis* (2015), *Secret of the Changeling* (2015), and *Flame of the Dragon* (2015).

Harrison, Paul. *Night of the Zombie Goldfish* **(Dr. Roach's Monstrous Stories series). Scholastic, 2012. Gr. 3–4.**

First line: "KABBOOOFFFF!"

The pitch: Judd Crank's latest science experiment, the Erupto-Fizz, goes up in "a cloud of thick, purple smoke." Judd spends all his free time in his garage laboratory, where he keeps his beloved goldfish. When his mother calls, Judd picks up the remains of the failed experiment and stores them in an empty fish-food container. Predictably, his neighbor Zak comes over and feeds the fish from that container. "Huge bubbles of gas shot to the surface of the water, then exploded in belches, sending clouds of purple smoke billowing across the laboratory." Zak runs away.

Reading selection: Read chapter 3, "Zombie Goldfish." The beautiful, peaceful goldfish have turned into big, dumb zombies that "can live on land and walk with their flippers." They escape Judd's garage and head into town, incredibly hungry. Continue reading chapter 4, "The Happy Haddock." The zombie goldfish enter a restaurant named the Happy Haddock. When the head waiter refuses to seat them because none of them are wearing a tie, they gobble his head. The head waiter manages to escape, but the zombie goldfish create chaos. "They nibbled napkins, chomped on chairs, gnawed people's knees, and bit their bottoms." The zombie goldfish next head to the fishing store where "the hunters had become the hunted, as the fish chased the fishermen." The chapter ends with the line: "The townspeople began to panic!"

Read-alike recommendations: Companion books in the series about larger-than-life animal mutations include *Attack of the Giant Hamster* (2012), *Frogosaurus vs. the Bog Monster* (2013), and *The Day the Mice Stood Still* (2013). Surprisingly, there is another series featuring zombie goldfish. The first title is *My Big Fat Zombie Goldfish* by Mo O'Hara (Feiwel & Friends, 2013). The sequels include *My Big Fat Zombie Goldfish: The Seaquel* (2014), *My Big Fat Zombie Goldfish: Fins of Fury* (2015), and the collection *Any Fin Is Possible / The Curse of the Cat of Kings / Sports-Day Showdown* (2016).

Kent, Derek Taylor. *Scary School.* Harper, 2011. Gr. 3–6.

First lines: "I suppose the proper way to start an introduction is *with* an introduction, so . . . Hello! My name is Derek the Ghost."

The pitch: Derek is a ghost because he died last year in science class when "one of Mr. Acidbath's experiments went terribly wrong." Derek learns that if you're a ghost, "it means you still have something left to accomplish." And since he's stuck haunting Scary School, his "accomplishment" is that he's writing this book. Scary School is a school where human kids attend with monsters, like zombies, vampires, and werewolves. "Studies have shown that the more scared children are, the better they learn." Principal Headcrusher finds out that Scary School will host this year's Ghoul Games. That's the good news. The bad news is that the winners get to eat the losers. And there's a good chance Scary School will lose. One of the students who might get eaten is the new kid Charles Nukid. He meets the faculty. There's Mrs. T, the school librarian who is a "twenty-foot *Tyrannosaurus rex* wearing a blue dress and a blue bonnet," Dr. Dragonbreath, an actual dragon, Nurse Hairymoles, a witch who cures students but at the same time gives them a new disease, and Ms. Fang. As in one fang.

Reading selection: Read chapter 2, "Ms. Fang." The chapter opens with the lines: "Ms. Fang is the nicest, sweetest teacher at Scary School. She only ate twelve kids last year." The other fifth-grade teacher, Dr. Dragonbreath, ate his entire class on the first day of the school year. When Ms. Fang told her class that they could call her Ms. Fangs, "Benny said with a smirk, 'But you only have *one* fang, Ms. Fangs. Shouldn't we call you Ms. *Fang*?'" Ms. Fang gets mad and sucks out all of Benny's blood. She apologizes to his lifeless body after she remembers she indeed has only one fang. When Wendy calls her Ms. Fangs, the teacher sucks out Wendy's blood. Derek the Ghost says, "Okay, there wasn't much of a life lesson to be learned there, but I guess sometimes bad things just happen for no good reason, and that's an important lesson in itself." The chapter ends with students calling Nurse Hairymoles to bring the two kids back to life.

Read-alike recommendations: Derek writes three more books about Scary School in *Monsters on the March* (2012), *The Northern Frights* (2013), and *Zillions of Zombies* (Derek Taylor Kent Books, 2015). The Tales from Lovecraft Middle School series by Charles Gilman also features a school where some of the teachers and students are monsters. Those titles are *Professor Gargoyle* (Quirk, 2012), *The Slither Sisters* (2013), *Teacher's Pest* (2013), and *Substitute Creature* (2013).

Lubar, David. *The Gloomy Ghost* (Monsteriffic Tales series). Starscape, 2014. Gr. 4–6.
First line: "Being little stinks."

The pitch: It also stinks to be dead. These are the words of Rory, a kid who claims that he's a normal kid, "except I'm a ghost kid." Rory is hiding from his family after he messed with the insides of their television. As soon as he connected some wiring, it went "ZZZZZAAAAP" and white smoke poured out of it. He died eating poison berries but he's not exactly dead. Rory is confused. He sets out to find other ghosts to get some answers. He heads to a place in town he admits that he doesn't know much about, just that it's haunted.

Reading selection: Read chapter 7, "Welcome?" Rory has made his way into the haunted Winston House and immediately sees four adult ghosts. They seem to be wearing old clothing, perhaps from the Pilgrim era. Those four ignore him while a ghost in another room keeps screaming at him. Rory decides, "I didn't care if there were answers here. The place was too creepy." As he's leaving, he meets the ghost of a girl and she says, "You're new." She also tells him that he's not dead . . . yet. He has two hours of life left in his body. Once that's gone, he'll be dead for good. Rory runs back home where his physical body is hidden in the bushes. The chapter ends with the lines: "It was 4:13. If I didn't get someone to find my body, I'd be dead by 6:13—dead forever."

Read-alike recommendations: This is just one of the Monsterrific Tales books about other kids in Rory's town of Lewington. Those titles are *The Vanishing Vampire* (2013), *Hyde and Shriek* (2013), *The Unwilling Witch* (2014), *The Wavering Werewolf* (2014), and *Bully Bug* (2014).

Lubar, David. *My Rotten Life* (Nathan Abercrombie, Accidental Zombie series). Starscape, 2009. Gr. 4–6.
First line: "It's no fun having your heart ripped from your body, slammed to the floor, and stomped into a puddle of quivering red mush."

The pitch: Nathan had his heart ripped, slammed, and stomped three times in one particularly bad day at school. The first was when the most popular girl publicly humiliated him in front of everyone. The second was when he was picked last in gym class, and the third was when everyone in art class learned he is a "vidiot"—a kid really, really bad at video games. Nathan decides, "If school stinks, then life stinks." A girl named Abigail offers to help him feel better. Nathan worries. "I wondered whether she was going to ask me to join some weird club or sing a happy song." Instead, Abigail takes Nathan to visit her scientist uncle Zardo, who is working on a "formula to get rid of unwanted feelings." Nathan's friend Mookie warns him by saying, "Science is dangerous. I've seen too many movies where people turn into insects because of science." Uncle Zardo gives Nathan a potion called "Hurt-Be-Gone," and that's when things get even worse. . . .

Reading selection: Read part of chapter 6, "The Inversion Diet," starting with the lines: "Mookie was there, waiting for me next to the front steps. 'You look awful,' he said." Nathan feels his stomach sloshing around. He starts to talk but out comes "Uuuhhhbluuuuppppuuuhhhuuubooorrruppp." He follows that with "a smaller burp. It lasted only about fifteen seconds." Mookie is convinced something is rotting inside of Nathan and instructs him to hang upside down on gymnastic bars. Something plops out. "'You have waffles for breakfast?' Mookie asked." The chapter ends with Mookie staring at Nathan's face. "'I'm pretty sure it's worse than you think,' he finally said. 'A whole lot worse.'"

Read-alike recommendations: The other titles in the series are *Dead Guy Spy* (2010), *Goop Soup* (2010), *The Big Stink* (2010), and *Enter the Zombie* (2011). *Undead Ed* by Rotterly Ghoulstone (Razorbill, 2010) is the story of a kid who wakes up as a zombie. Its sequels are *Undead Ed and the Demon Freakshow* (2013) and *Undead Ed and the Fingers of Doom* (2014).

McGeddon, R. *Zombies!* (Disaster Diaries series). Imprint, 2016. Gr. 4–6.

First line: "Professor Pamplemousse was a small man by anyone's standards."

The pitch: Professor Pamplemousse, the science teacher, is not respected by any of his students. Most of the kids "towered several inches above him." While trying to give one final science lesson during the "final few minutes of the final day of the final week of the school term," he fails to attract the attention of Sam and Arty. The two boys are goofing off, trying to come up with ideas on how to prank Arty's brother Jesse. Arty doesn't get along with his brother because "first, Arty's older brother wasn't very nice, and second, Arty's brother wasn't very nice." They decide to throw water balloons at Jesse. (Sam nixed Arty's idea of feeding Jesse to a shark.) Professor Pamplemousse is surprised his science experiment turns purple instead of green. The test tube explodes, coating a kid named Simon. As the students lead a countdown to the beginning of summer vacation, Simon "was left to undergo an un-deadly transformation." Sam and Arty are joined by Emmie and Phoebe. They notice six figures shuffling toward them.

Reading selection: Read the second half of chapter 4, starting with the line: "'They're z-z-z-,' Arty stuttered. 'Z-z-z—' 'Zombies,' Sam whispered." The kids run and hide in the park's playhouse. They find Professor Pamplemousse whimpering. Sam tells him, "You're not going to believe what's happened," to which Professor Pamplemousse replies, "Everyone's started turning into zombies and they're trying to eat everyone else?" Sam nods. "Okay, maybe you will believe it." It turns out the professor was trying to mix a new lotion for his sore knee and accidentally created a zombie potion. He says, "It went a bit wrong," and the narrator says, "Pamplemousse was definitely a contender for the International Understatement of the Year award." They are all attacked by the local butcher, who has been turned into a zombie. The chapter ends with the line: "Pamplemousse blinked in surprise as Mr. Gristle raised his blood-soaked cleaver above his head and prepared to swing."

Read-alike recommendations: Two more titles in the series are *Aliens!* (2016) and *Brainwashed!* (2016). *Zombiekins* by Kevin Bolger (Razorbill, 2010) is about a zombie stuffed animal plush toy. More zombies can be found in *The Zombie Chasers* by John Kloepfer (HarperCollins, 2010) and its sequels: *Undead Ahead* (2011), *Sludgement Day* (2012), *Empire State of Slime* (2013), *Nothing Left to Ooze* (2014), *Zombies of the Caribbean* (2014), and *World Zombination* (2015).

Scieszka, Jon, ed. *Terrifying Tales* (Guys Read series). Walden Pond, 2015. Gr. 4–7.

First lines: "Come on in. Closer. Don't be afraid. It's just a bunch of stories. What could be so terrifying about that?"

The pitch: The first story in this "terrifying" collection of short stories features an imaginary friend who turns out to be pure evil. The sweet old lady in the second story is anything but sweet. She casts curses on neighborhood kids left and right. And the third story in this book? The narrator starts out by stating, "I'm going to tell you the scariest, bloodiest, most messed-up story I have ever heard. It will probably make you pee in your pants." This collection of scary stories was edited by Jon Scieszka, the guy who wrote *The Stinky Cheeseman and Other Fairly Stupid Tales*, the Time Warp Trio series, and other funny books. Mr. Scieszka doesn't crack his usual jokes this time around, however. He wants kids to be scared. There are ten horrific stories including one by R. L. Stine, the

Goosebumps guy, and even Dav Pilkey, the Captain Underpants author. Here's one by author Kelly Barnhill.

Reading selection: Read "Don't Eat the Baby." The kid in this story makes a wish at a very special wishing well. He wishes for a brother. Begin reading halfway through the story with the sentence: "I woke up with a yelp." The narrator is excited to find a new brother under his bed. The brother doesn't want the rest of the family to know he's there yet. He's also hungry all the time. "He coughed and something yellow flew out of his mouth. Like a piece of paper. Or a feather. When I got home later that day, I realized that my canary was missing." The new brother goes to school with the narrator. The class hamster goes missing. "That's when I started to get suspicious." End the passage with the sentence: "*That's it,* I thought."

Read-alike recommendations: This is the sixth volume of the Guys Read anthologies. The other collections are *Guys Write for Guys Read* (2005), *Funny Business* (2010), *Thriller* (2011), *The Sports Page* (2012), and *Other Worlds* (2013).

Towell, Katy. *Charlie and the Grandmothers.* Knopf, 2015. Gr. 4–6.

First line: "Charlie was awake."

The pitch: One reason twelve-year-old Charlie is awake is because he's noticed "all the children in town were disappearing, and Charlie knew that his sister and he were next." The children leave town, and the adults are told the missing kids are away visiting their grandmothers. Nobody seems to care that none of them ever return. Nobody, except Charlie. Perhaps he's just a worrier. Charlie worries about floods on cloudless nights and wildfires during thunderstorms. His sister Georgie, on the other hand, isn't afraid of anything. Her motto seems to be: "When adventure comes calling, how can an adventurer say no?" Charlie fears sleep and he does his best to stay awake. He knows trouble comes at night.

Reading selection: Read the middle of chapter 1, "Charlie and Georgie," with the line: "But then came the darkest night of all." Charlie is reading a book when "he saw, to his great alarm, nothing." No lights from the streetlamps outside, no light from the moon, "and while he watched, the very stars went out." Charlie's lamp goes out, "leaving him in blackness with a thundering heart." He hears voices from his mother's bedroom. His mother is muttering, "They should . . . experience . . . the world." A second voice, "a strange whispering voice only just audible to the sort of person who makes a practice of listening for strange voices," replies, "Happy! So happy! No need for kiddies!" Charlie wakes his sister and the two head for their mother's bedroom. She is alone and wakes up wondering what's going on. The lights outside come back on. Outside their window, a few yards from their apartment, is an old woman, staring and grinning at Charlie. The chapter ends with Charlie gasping and closing the curtains. "'It's just some old rag-and-bone woman,' he told himself. 'Isn't there anything in the world I'm not afraid of?'"

Read-alike recommendations: Granny by Anthony Horowitz (Puffin, 2009) features a scary grandmother and is written in a lighter tone than *Charlie and the Grandmothers.* Holly Grant's *The League of Beastly Dreadfuls* (Random House, 2015) follows the story of Anastasia who is sent to live with two great-aunts in their home—a former asylum. Its sequel is *The Dastardly Deed* (2016).

Zombie, Zack. *A Scare of a Dare* (Diary of a Minecraft Zombie series). Harbine, 2015. Gr. 3–5.

First line: "Uuuuurrrgghhhh!!!"

The pitch: Apparently that's the sound a zombie kid makes when his mother tells him to get up because it's nighttime and "those villagers aren't going to scare themselves." To which the zombie kid says again, "Uuuuurrgghhhh!!!" Zombie Mom has had it. "Don't *Uuuuurrgghhhh* Me. You get up, and ready this instant!" A young Minecraft Zombie shares his diary. Zombie kids need to stay out of the sun, not brush their teeth, and to eat their rotten meatloaf. This zombie goes to Scare School with his best friends Creepy, Skelee, and Slimey. Our zombie also has a good sense of humor. When he asks his mom where zombies come from, "She seemed a bit tongue tied. But then I remembered she doesn't have a tongue!" His mother recovers enough to inform him that zombies are created by computers to make the game Minecraft more challenging. Our zombie is also interested in a zombie girl named Sally Cadaver. He wonders how "I'm supposed to kiss her with no lips."

Reading selection: Read the third Wednesday entry. It starts with the sentence: "Today I got caught passing a note to Skelee in class." His teacher catches the note and reads it aloud to the whole class. It says, "I LIKE SALLY CADAVER AND I WANT HER TO BE MY GIRLFRIEND." Our zombie feels his life is over. "The only thing that saved me was that Sally was out for a week because she was getting her tonsils put back in." He's worried about a zombie kid named Jeff, who is also interested in Sally Cadaver. Jeff has matured faster than the other zombie kids. "Jeff was the first to grow mold on his chest." The chapter ends with our zombie convinced that Sally will go out with Jeff. "I'm doomed."

Read-alike recommendations: The other titles in the series include *Bullies and Buddies* (2015), *When Nature Calls* (2015), *A Zombie Swap* (2015), *School Daze* (2015), *Zombie Goes to Camp* (2015), *Zombie Family Reunion* (2015), *Back to Scare School* (2015), *Zombie's Birthday Apocalypse* (2015), and *One Bad Apple* (2016).

CHAPTER 5

Science Fiction

Science fiction has grown in popularity mostly due to dystopian settings like Lois Lowry's book *The Giver* and the Hunger Game series by Suzanne Collins, stories about things gone wrong in our world. Science fiction is also popular because of stories about aliens, space travel, and anything else that can be explained by science, no matter how implausible it may be.

Beaty, Andrea. *Attack of the Fluffy Bunnies*. Amulet, 2010. Gr. 3–6.

First lines: "Meanwhile, in space . . . The flaming meteor hurtled through the endless, black void. Remember this. It's important later."

The pitch: Fluffs are Fierce, Large, Ugly, and Ferocious Furballs. Enormous fierce warrior rabbits "whose long, floppy ears are for slapping. Whose long, floppy feet are for stomping. And whose large eyes spin in opposite directions to hypnotize unsuspecting prey. Oh yeah, and they have fangs." In other words, "FLUFFS = BAD." The flaming meteor had crashed into the Fluffs' marshmallow planet. The Fluffs escaped and headed for Earth. Twins Joules and Kevin Rockman are attending Camp Whatsitooya nestled on the shores of Lake Whatsosmelly. They aren't all that crazy about being there. But it's better than attending the International SPAMathon with their parents.

Reading selection: Read chapter 9. The twins are hiking in the woods. Kevin feels that something is watching them. He is a movie buff. He realizes that he's acting like Annoying Movie Character Number 1, who says things like: "I feel like someone's watching me." And then getting "eaten by the thing that is actually watching them." Annoying Movie Character Number 1 is also known for producing great screams. The twins hear rustling in the undergrowth followed by a noise that sounds like "Grmmblemrrrmm." Joules pokes a stick in the weeds, and three large bunnies with blackened rumps run by. The kids are relieved, forgetting that rabbits should not be the size of dogs. The chapter ends with eyes watching the kids. "Six of them, to be exact. All of them swirly."

Read-alike recommendations: The adventure continues in the sequel *Fluffy Bunnies 2: The Schnoz of Doom* (2015). *Wuv Bunnies from Outers Pace* by David Elliott (Holiday House, 2008) follows two space rabbits that save children from being turned into carrots.

Bransford, Nathan. *Jacob Wonderbar and the Cosmic Space Kapow.* Dial, 2011. Gr. 4–6.

First line: "Each type of substitute teacher had its own special weakness, and Jacob Wonderbar knew every possible trick to distract them."

The pitch: Jacob sizes up the new sub. "She was impossibly tall and thin, with a wart on both cheeks and a glint of evil in her eye. . . . She had a crooked set of yellow teeth and foul breath that smelled like burned coffee and rotten eggs." She's the scariest substitute teacher Jacob has ever seen and she knows all about his reputation. She warns him, "I'm watching you." Her coffee mug gets broken, Jacob sets off the fire sprinkler and soaks the sub, Jacob and his friends Dexter and Sarah get sent to the office, they trade an alien a corn dog for his spaceship, and fly off into outer space. That's the short version.

Reading selection: Read chapter 7. It opens with the line: "'There goes Mars!' Dexter shouted as the red planet rushed past the window." The kids' new spaceship takes them throughout the solar system in a short amount of time. They are powerless to alter their course. Jupiter zooms by, then Saturn, Uranus, Neptune, and Pluto. They leave the solar system, dodge a star, and head straight toward a random planet. The kids shoot missiles at it and then circle with a slingshot effect to cause the planet to collide with the star. Explosion after explosion follows. Jacob finds the brakes and the trio reflects on all that happened. "Stars had exploded. Planets had been obliterated. The sky was streaked with star guts." The chapter ends with Dexter finding his voice. "I think we just broke the universe."

Read-alike recommendations: Jacob returns in two sequels: *Jacob Wonderbar for President of the Universe* (2012) and *Jacob Wonderbar and the Interstellar Time Warp* (2013). *Cosmic* by Frank Cottrell Boyce (Walden Pond, 2010) is the story of Liam, who informs his parents that he's not attending the South Lakeland Outdoor Activity Center. Instead, he's in outer space.

Evans, Richard Paul. *The Prisoner of Cell 25* **(Michael Vey series). Simon Pulse, 2011. Gr. 6–7.**

First line: "Have you found the last two?"

The pitch: There is a million-dollar bounty out on two children. One of them might be fourteen-year-old Michael, a high school student who is bullied because of his size and also because of his Tourette's syndrome. He has just been shoved inside his locker upside down by Jack and his flunkies. Weirdly, Michael is the one who has to serve detention. Principal Dallstrom, who does not "put the PAL in principal," has it in for Michael after overhearing our young hero say that Medusa, the mythological character who turns people into stone with her stare, was Mr. Dallstrom's "great-great-great-great-grandmother." Is there any reason to believe that Michael is one of the hunted children? Short, bullied Michael? What's so special about him?

Reading selection: Read the second half of chapter 4, "The Cheerleader." Start with the ominous sentence: "I had just come around the corner of the school when Jack and his posse, Mitchell and Wade, emerged from between two Dumpsters." Mitchell hits Michael in the eye. Jack orders him to hit Michael again. "The next fist landed on my nose. It hurt like crazy. I could feel blood running down my lips and chin. My eyes watered. Then Jack walked up and punched me right in the gut." The trio then try to pants poor Michael. A cheerleader named Taylor yells at the bullies to stop, but they ignore her and continue to torment Michael. As the boys tug at his pants, Michael feels a surge of anger go through his body. "Suddenly, a sharp, electric *ZAP!* pierced the air like the sound of ice being dropped onto a hot griddle. Electricity flashed and Jack and his posse screamed out as they all fell to their backs and flopped about on the grass like fish on land." Michael warns them, "Next time you bully me, or any of my friends, I'll triple it." When Michael looks up, he sees that Taylor has seen everything. Michael realizes that this is "bad, bad news."

Read-alike recommendations: The other titles in the series are *Rise of the Elgan* (2012), *Battle of the Ampere* (2013), *Hunt for the Jade Dragon* (2014), *Storm of Lightning* (2015), and *Fall of Hades* (2016). *Bounders* by Monica Tesler (Aladdin, 2016) is a science fiction novel about a bullied kid who is recruited by Earth Force to fight aliens.

Falls, Kat. *Dark Life.* **Scholastic, 2010. Gr. 5–7.**

First lines: "I peered into the deep-sea canyon, hoping to spot a toppled skyscraper. Maybe even the Statue of Liberty."

The pitch: Ty and his family are underwater pioneers. They, like others, choose to farm deep below the ocean's surface after natural disasters have destroyed most of Earth's land. Topsiders, those survivors who still live on the continents, are squeezed together, "hundreds of thousands of people into a single square mile." Ty meets a Topsider, Gemma, who is searching for her missing brother. Both of them are in danger from outlaws, escaped convicts from an experimental maximum security prison. This gang has begun targeting underwater communities. Ty comes face-to-face with the leader of the outlaws, an albino named Shade.

Reading selection: Before reading, explain that Ty is exploring an underwater home vandalized by a gang known as the Seablite Gang. Read the last portion of chapter 8, beginning with the sentence: "The power was back on." Ty sees a corpse floating in the water. "Inside the helmet, the dead man's pallid, hairless head gleamed as if lamprey eels had sucked out every drop of his blood. His skin was whiter than white. Except for his eyes, which were entirely black." The chapter ends with Ty shocked to learn the corpse is Shade. "And he was very much alive." Continue to read the entire short chapter 9. Shade shoots a harpoon at Ty, who manages to barely escape. An exhausted Ty looks around to see if he has been followed. The passage ends with the line: "There was no telltale glow of a helmet light anywhere—only endless midnight blue water."

Read-alike recommendations: The sequel, *Rip Tide* (2011), follows Ty and Gemma as they try to solve the mystery of an underwater community chained to a sunken submarine. The Caretaker Trilogy by David Klass is an ecological disaster science fiction trilogy for slightly older readers. The individual books in this series are *Firestorm* (Frances Foster, 2006), *Whirlwind* (2008), and *Timelock* (2009).

McDougall, Sophia. *Mars Evacuees.* Harper, 2015. Gr. 4–6.

First line: "When the polar ice advanced as far as Nottingham, my school was closed and I was evacuated to Mars."

The pitch: Alien invaders called Morrors have frozen most of the planet. Twelve-year-old Alice Dare is the daughter of a famous space fighter. Alice and a few hundred kids are sent to Mars to train for battle against these aliens. Earth forces are that desperate to send twelve-year-olds into the military. Mars hasn't completely transformed to support human life yet. "They'd been terraforming it for years and years, but even after everything they'd squirted or sprayed or puffed at it and all the money they'd spent on toasting it gently like a gigantic scone, still you could only *sort of* breathe the air and *sort of* not get sunburned to death." When Alice arrives on Mars, she and the others are taught by robot teachers. One kid finds a strange creature outside and gives a drawing of it to a girl named Josephine. Alice and Josephine take the drawing to a scientist named Dr. Muldoon.

Reading selection: Read the last third of chapter 8, beginning with the sentence: "Gavin started making exploding noises at Josephine at lunch, and after about a second's hesitation, Lilly joined in." After Alice and Josephine leave some bullies behind, they approach Dr. Muldoon. She looks at the drawing of the creature and says, "Are those *eyes*? Good lord, look at its *teeth*. You've got a nicely gruesome imagination, I'll give you kids that—flying worms at the bottom of the garden, it's brilliant." The girls convince her the creature is real and perhaps was sent by the Morrors. The chapter ends with the lines: "We all waited for Dr. Muldoon to get back to us. Only she didn't. Because after that, all of the adults disappeared."

Read-alike recommendations: Alice Dare returns in a sequel titled *Space Hostages* (2016). *Mike Stellar, Nerves of Steel* by K. A. Holt (Random House, 2009) is another science fiction book that discusses terraforming Mars.

Oakes, Cory Putnam. *Dinosaur Boy.* **Sourcebooks Jabberwocky, 2015. Gr. 3–6.**

First line: "It all started with a bump."

The pitch: Sawyer started growing two lines of bumps down his back one summer. Then his tail started growing. Sawyer wasn't totally surprised. "After all, my grandfather was part stegosaurus. And everybody knows that dinosaur skips a generation." His mother is pleased. She brags to relatives that her son has the dinosaur gene. It hurts to grow a tail. It feels like landing on your tailbone. Sawyer starts craving fruits and vegetables. "Plates and plates of vegetables. Plus salads so big I had to put them in mixing bowls." When Sawyer's tail grows "four-foot-long, razor-sharp spikes," he has to be particularly cautious. "I shredded two rugs and the side of the couch, plus I did untold damage to the wood floor in the entryway before my dad had the idea of skewering a tennis ball onto the end of each spike." Sawyer is about to start fifth grade. He worries about being teased, "plates, tail, spikes, and all." While Sawyer is sitting in science class with his best friend Elliot, he notices a kid named Allan up to no good.

Reading selection: Read chapter 4, "Butt Brain," beginning with the sentence: "Like Elliot, Allan had been in my class since kindergarten." Sawyer and Allan are not friends. Allan and some kids are looking up different kinds of dinosaurs. They laugh when they announce that Sawyer is a stegosaurus. Sawyer mutters, "I could have told you that." The kids read aloud information that the stegosaurus had a brain the size of a walnut. When they learn that it might have had a supplementary brain in its hindquarters, another kid named Parker starts chanting, "Butt Brain! Butt Brain!" The new principal, Mrs. Mathis, walks in yelling, "SILENCE!" She takes Parker with her, telling him, "Bring your things. You shan't be returning." The chapter ends with Parker looking "very small and pathetic as he exchanged a miserable look with Allan and then followed Principal Mathis out of the door."

Read-alike recommendations: The sequel is *Dinosaur Boy Saves Mars* (2016). The Creature from 7th Grade series by Bob Balaban features a seventh grader who turns into an eight-foot-tall dinosaur during school. The two titles in the series are *Boy or Beast* (Viking, 2012) and *Sink or Swim* (2013).

Sparkes, Ali. *Spider Stampede* **(S.W.I.T.C.H. series). Darby Creek, 2013. Gr. 3–5.**

First lines: "AARRGGHH!!!! GETITOFF! GETITOFF! GETITOFF-MEEEE!!!!"

The pitch: Eight-year-old Danny doesn't do well with creepy crawlers. He is currently wearing nothing but his swimming trunks and a spider. His twin brother, Josh, actually loves all things in nature including bugs and critters like

spiders. Danny admits that his brother is good for "creepy-crawler removal." He still remembers when he "screamed loud enough to wake the dead after stepping into his brother's box of centipedes when he got up to go to the bathroom in the middle of the night." The two brothers chase their dog Piddle (he got his name "after a habit he had when he got over-excited") who runs from their yard and leads them into their strange neighbor's secret laboratory. They head back home and discover their legs are covered with a strange liquid. They begin to wash it off in their bathroom when something creepy begins happening to them.

Reading selection: Begin reading a few pages into the chapter titled "Too Many Knees" with the sentence: "Then the bath started to grow." The boys feel strange. They catch their reflection in the shower attachment. "In it Danny saw something huge and hairy and standing high on eight legs. It had eight eyes and a rather surprised expression. And it MUST BE RIGHT ON TOP OF HIM!!!!!" The boys realize they have been turned into two spiders. Continue reading a few pages into the next chapter titled "A Hairy Experience." They hear a scream. Their sister Jenny sees two spiders in the bathtub and takes off her sandal. End the selection with the line: "They were about to be pulped."

Read-alike recommendations: The twins are transformed into different species of the animal kingdom in each volume of the S.W.I.T.C.H. series. Those titles are *Fly Frenzy* (2013), *Grasshopper Glitch* (2013), *Ant Attack* (2013), *Crane Fly Crash* (2013), *Beetle Blast* (2013), *Frog Freakout* (2014), *Newt Nemesis* (2014), *Lizard Loopy* (2014), *Chameleon Chaos* (2014), *Turtle Terror* (2014), *Gecko Gladiator* (2014), *Anaconda Adventure* (2014), and *Alligator Action* (2014).

Tobin, Paul. *How to Capture an Invisible Cat* **(Genius Factor series). Bloomsbury, 2016. Gr. 4–6.**

First line: "Let's just say the cat was bigger than a horse."

The pitch: Delphine is a witty young troublemaker who once bought $24 worth of shaving cream and sprayed a three-foot layer of it on her brother's bedroom floor. She also argued with her friend Liz over the merits of cake versus pie, and her mother got mad "even though the table was fine once we put it back into place and Liz's glasses didn't break when I knocked them off with the pillow and the bite mark on my shoulder cleared up after only a couple of days." Delphine makes friends with Nate, also known as Egghead, who is possibly the smartest kid in the whole wide world. He taught his dog how to talk. Maybe not all that well. The dog is limited to saying things like "stick" and its name, "Bosper," but still, the dog *is* talking.

Reading selection: Read the first half of chapter 1. Delphine states that an invisible cat the size of a horse is trying to kill her. She goes on to tell how she and Nate "became friends, and that his invisible cat almost killed me. Sort of. It's a long story that starts with dogs." Nate informs Delphine that he "accelerated" his dog Bosper, but not all that well. "'His tongue's not optimized for speaking. Our own mouths and tongues have been shaped for speech by evolution.' 'Bosper has a bad mouth!' the dog said." Nate has also built a mechanical dog nose that allows him to heighten his own ability to detect smells. He learns that Delphine smells like a friend. The passage ends with the sentence: "Anyway, that's how Nathan Bannister and I became friends."

Read-alike recommendations: The second book in the series is *How to Outsmart a Billion Robot Bees* (2017). *The Flinkwater Factor* by Pete Hautman (Simon & Schuster, 2015) follows Ginger Crump as she tries to save the day with the help of a boy genius and a talking dog. Its sequel is *The Forgetting Machine* (2016).

Trine, Greg. *Willy Maykit in Space.* Houghton Mifflin Harcourt, 2015. Gr. 3–5.

First lines: "When Willy Maykit was three years old, his father went on an African safari and came home with amazing stories of lions, tigers, and bears. Or at least lions, elephants, and hippos. There are no tigers or bears in Africa. But they're doing fine in the elephant and hippo department."

The pitch: Fourth grader Willy Maykit misses his explorer father who went missing on one of his trips. We learn that he was captured not by headhunters but by foothunters. That's right, foothunters. Willy's class goes on a field trip into space to Planet Ed. It's a new planet that was discovered by a school janitor named Ed. Willy gets separated from the rest of the class and they leave without him. He is accompanied by a seagull named Phelps. Willy learns that another student, a girl he likes named Cindy, was also left behind. They are joined by an alien named Norp who was left behind on his planet's school trip. Norp warns Willy and Cindy that nice-looking Planet Ed is home to monsters that come out at night.

Reading selection: Read the beginning of chapter 8, "Something Big and Hairy This Way Comes." A monster that looks like Bigfoot on steroids chases the kids. Phelps swoops down and lands bird poop in the monster's eyes, allowing them all to escape. As Norp leads them into the forest, Willy asks, "Where are you taking us?" End this section with the lines: "A safe place. Trust me." Move over to chapter 10,

"Three's Company," to read a short two-page passage. Begin with the lines: "'And lucky that Phelps came along when he did,' Cindy said. 'That monster didn't know what hit him.'" We learn that the monster's name is Sam. He is grossed out by having bird poop land in his eye. The other monsters find out what happened to Sam and make fun of him. "All of the other monsters laughed and called him names. They wouldn't let poor Sam join in any monster games." End the reading with the lines: "So now he wanted revenge. *If it's the last thing I do*, he said to himself."

Read-alike recommendations: The Moon Base Alpha series by Stuart Gibbs features kids traveling in space. The first title is *Space Case* (Simon & Schuster, 2014) and opens with the line: "Let's get something straight right off the bat: Everything the movies have ever taught you about space travel is garbage." Its sequel is *Spaced Out* (2016).

Yancey, Rick. *The 5th Wave.* Putnam, 2013. Gr. 6–7.

First line: "Aliens are stupid."

The pitch: Actually, aliens are not stupid. They are smart enough to exterminate most of the human population through a series of strategic attacks. The 1st Wave knocked out everything electrical, including planes in flight. The 2nd Wave created tsunamis to wipe out the coastlines and pack the survivors inland. The 3rd Wave unleashed a pestilence, and what happens with the 4th Wave is mind blowing. Cassie is a teenage girl who has lost both parents. Her younger brother Sam was taken away from her. She is hiding in the woods, worried the aliens, or the Others as she calls them, will spot her with their drones. "I can describe in detail every leaf and twig in this stretch of forest. I have no clue what's out there beyond these woods and the two-mile stretch of interstate I hike every week to forage for supplies. I'm guessing a lot more of the same: abandoned towns reeking of sewage and rotting corpses, burned-out shells of houses, feral dogs and cats, pileups that stretch for miles on the highway. And bodies. Lots and lots of bodies." This is Cassie's new world as she waits for the Others to unleash the 5th Wave. On one of her forages to a gas station, she learns she is not alone.

Reading selection: Read chapter 4. Cassie encounters a wounded soldier pointing a gun at her. She refuses his order to drop her weapon, and he finally drops his. Cassie demands the soldier hold up his hidden hand. When he raises his bloody hand, Cassie notices "something long and thin and metallic, and my fingers yanked back on the trigger, and the rifle kicked against my shoulder hard, and the barrel bucked in my hand as I emptied the clip." The chapter ends with Cassie inspecting what the dead soldier has in his hand. "It was a crucifix."

Read-alike recommendations: The 5th Wave is the first book in a trilogy that includes *The Infinite Sea* (2014) and *The Last Star* (2016). *Alien Invasion and Other Inconveniences* by Brian Yansky (Candlewick, 2010) opens with the line: "It takes less time for them to conquer the world than it takes me to brush my teeth." Its sequel is *Homicidal Aliens and Other Disappointments* (2013).

CHAPTER 6

Superheroes (and Supervillains)

While compiling the list of science fiction books, I was surprised to see how many recently published books there are about the subcategory of superheroes and supervillains, enough so to make this separate category. What kid doesn't dream of having a superpower?

Anderson, John David. *Minion.* **Walden Pond, 2014. Gr. 4–7.**

First line: "When I was twelve years old, give or take, my father strapped a bomb to my chest and drove me to the First National Bank and Trust so we could steal $27,500."

The pitch: The father and son duo succeed in robbing that bank. Michael's father stole that exact amount because he only steals what he needs and, as Michael says, "He needed $27,500 to finish one of his projects and to buy groceries. We were out of frozen waffles." Michael's father adopted him from St. Mary of the Woods School for Wayward Boys. Michael has a special talent, "a little abracadabra." He can sort of hypnotize folks. He tells the reader, "It's okay if you don't believe me. Just look into my eyes and I'll convince you." Michael's father hopes that his son becomes trilingual: fluent in English, Spanish, and "Mad Scientistese." Things change when both father and son find themselves in the world of superheroes and supervillains.

Reading selection: Start reading halfway into the first chapter with the sentence: "My power just came to me, gradual, like how fingernails grow." It just happened. Michael didn't get bitten by a radioactive bug or "fall into a toilet transporting me to an alternative dimension where I was actually a demigod sent to the planet earth or any load of bull like that." He goes on to give examples of his power. At St. Mary's, he convinced Sister Margaret that he needed double portions of pudding. Another time, he made Sister Beatrice break-dance. Michael explains that he didn't use his power to make people adopt him. He wanted someone who truly wanted him. End the passage with the sentence: "Which is why I stared down at my shoes the day Dad came to St. Mary's, looking, he said, for someone who could help him take over the world."

Read-alike recommendation: The companion novel to *Minion* is *Sidekicked* (2013), the story of a middle school kid who possesses super senses: "his hearing, sight, taste, touch, and smell are most powerful on the planet."

Bacon, Lee. *Joshua Dread.* Delacorte, 2012. Gr. 4–6.

First line: "Our class got out of sixth period early the day my parents tried to flood the earth."

The pitch: Joshua's parents are the supervillains known as the Dread Duo. Mom is the Botanist. She can control plants as well as zombies. Dad is Dr. Dread, an inventor with superpowered eyesight. Before they decided to destroy with world with the Weather Alterator, they had previously unleashed their zombie horde on the nation's capital and "tried to vaporize California with a death laser." To keep up with the latest knowledge of all things evil, they attend the Vile Fair, a yearly "kind of supervillain convention that happened every year in New York City." Back home, Joshua doesn't want any of his classmates to know that the Dread Duo are really his parents. He also doesn't want his parents to destroy the world. Joshua worries they will get hurt by the nation's most popular superhero, Captain Justice. The Dread Duo trap a group of journalists and a busload of school children, including Joshua, in their Vortex of Silence. They threaten to unleash severe weather if they don't receive a private jet filled with hundred-dollar bills.

Reading selection: Read chapter 2. Captain Justice has arrived and tells the Dread Duo "how unpleasant it is to see you again." He rips the roof off the school bus to free the children but a little girl informs him, "The bus driver said it wasn't safe for us to go outside the Vortex of Silence on foot. Because of the storm and all." Captain Justice hadn't thought of that and throws the bus roof through the front wall of the post office. Just as Captain Justice is about to crush Dr. Dread, Joshua yells out and asks Captain Justice for a picture. The vain superhero agrees, giving Joshua's parents time to escape. Captain Justice proclaims, "Another shameful plot has been foiled by Captain Justice!" He tells the children to eat their Frosted Fuel Flakes, a product he endorses. "And then he launched into the air, vanishing into the blue, cloudless sky."

Read-alike recommendations: There are two sequels: *The Nameless Hero* (2013) and *The Dominion Key* (2014). *The Cloak Society* by Jeramey Kraatz (Full Fathom Five, 2012) opens with the line: "You don't just fall into villainy." Alex is a young supervillain who starts questioning his role.

Jensen, Marion. *Almost Super*. **Harper, 2014. Gr. 4–6.**

First line: "I woke up on the worst day of my entire life fully expecting it to be the best day of my entire life."

The pitch: What happened on the worst day of Rafter Bailey's life was that someone gave Great-Aunt Silva Matilda some fizzy lemonade. And the fizzy lemonade caused Great-Aunt Silva Matilda to burp. And Great-Aunt Silva Matilda breathes fire, so when she burped she set the drapes on fire. Cousin Jack put out the flames by shooting a stream of water from his palms. Grandpa directed Rafter to point Great-Aunt Silva Matilda toward the fireplace. "She'll likely be burping up a storm all afternoon," he said. The Baileys all have superpowers. Grandpa has super strength. Rafter's father can fly. Rafter and his brother Benny will soon be of age to get their superpowers. That's why Rafter expects it to be the best day of his entire life. What makes it the worst day of his entire life? Check the title of the book.

Reading selection: Read a few pages into chapter 2, "I'm Always Afraid of Getting Lava down My Tights," with the sentences: "'Benny,' Dad said. 'You got your power first. What is it? What is your ability?'" Benny doesn't want to tell his family but finally whispers, "I can turn my belly button from an innie to an outie." The family is stunned while Benny demonstrates. "With a soft pop, his belly button popped out of his stomach." He then reverses this power and says, "Ta-da" weakly. Rafter's superpower is just as lame. He can light matches on polyester. When Benny complains that Great-Aunt Silva Matilda's belches are more powerful than they are, Grandpa tells them to stop bellyaching and says that when things look horrible, "a superhero stands, turns so he can look evil right in the eyes, and says, 'Is that the best you can do?'" End the reading with the line: "Grandpa turned and left the room."

Read-alike recommendations: The sequel is *Searching for Super* (2015). The Extraordinary Adventures of Ordinary Boy series by William Boniface features a kid named Ordinary Boy because he is the only one in the city without superpowers. Those titles in this series are *The Hero Revealed* (2006), *The Return of Meteor Boy?* (2008), and *The Great Powers Outage* (2008).

Leung, Bryce, and Kristy Shen. *Little Miss Evil*. **Spencer Hill, 2015. Gr. 4–6.**

First line: "When your dad's a cackling super-villain, you get some pretty weird stuff for your birthday."

The pitch: Fiona opened a present and found a real samurai sword—for her six-year-old birthday. She got a Universal Remote Detonator a few years later. "Point it at any electronic device and it blows the device to smithereens." For her thirteenth birthday, Fiona gets a bionic flamethrower. She tries it out and promptly burns her father's workbench. Her father thinks it will make her more popular at school but Fiona corrects him. The other kids are already freaked out by her. "I ride to school in a helicopter, I live in a giant hollowed-out volcano, and my dad is Manson Ng, evil super-villain extraordinaire who regularly terrorizes the town just to show he can." He wants to prepare her to one day take over the family business. Fiona has other plans and tells him, "I. Don't. Want. To. Be. A. Super. Villain!"

Reading selection: Read the very end of chapter 1, where Fiona says, "Dad, you never did answer my question." She wants to know why he thinks it's important she gets a flamethrower now. Before he can answer, the ceiling crashes down on them and the air-raid sirens go off. Continue reading the first part of chapter 2. They are being attacked by another supervillain's army. Fiona complains, "This is turning out to be the worst birthday." An explosion knocks her to the floor and she's confronted by a man who shoves a gun in her face. End the selection where the man says, "Look who I've found."

Read-alike recommendations: The Vordak the Incomprehensible series by Scott Seegert includes instructions on how to be evil. The first book in the series is *How to Grow Up and Rule the World* (Egmont USA, 2010). The other books are *Rule the School* (2011), *Double Trouble* (2012), and *Time Travel Trouble* (2013).

Lewis, Josh. *Super Chicken Nugget Boy and the Furious Fry*. Hyperion, 2010. Gr. 3–4.

First lines: "It was 10:43 in the morning in Gordonville. At Bert Lahr Elementary, everyone was doing all the things they did every school day."

The pitch: What Dirk does every school day is bully the other kids with his sidekick Snort. He gets away with it because his dad is the principal. Dirk has mastered the art of whining. He orders his father to send kids to detention. When he doesn't get his way, Dirk makes his mother yell at his father. The new kid Fern comes up with a plan to stop Dirk. He dresses up as a new superhero, Super Chicken Nugget Boy, to scare Dirk. Things go

awry when Fern, dressed up as a giant chicken nugget, falls into a mysterious "green gooey liquid in the grungy, above-the-ground-pool-type thingy."

Reading selection: Read most of chapter 10, "I Love Goo, Goo Loves Me." Dirk and Snort show up looking for Fern. They are about to hit Fern's friend Lester when Fern, now a real, enormous Super Chicken Nugget Boy, confronts the bullies. He bumps Snort with his hip and "Bonk! Snort went flying across the alley." He flips Dirk with his foot, sending the bully flying through the air. He threatens to drop Dirk into the green gooey liquid until Dirk promises to stop picking on kids. End the selection where Dirk grabs Snort and they run away with a *"Snort! Snort! Snort! Snort! Snort!"*

Read-alike recommendations: The story continues with *Super Chicken Nugget Boy vs. Dr. Ned-Grant and His Eggplant Army* (2010), *Super Chicken Nugget Boy and the Pizza Planet People* (2011), and *Super Chicken Nugget Boy and the Massive Meatloaf Man Manhunt* (2011).

Marko, Cyndi. *Let's Get Cracking!* (Kung Pow Chicken series). Scholastic, 2014. Gr. 3–4.

First line: "Gordon Blue seemed like an ordinary chicken."

The pitch: Gordon was indeed ordinary until he and his little brother Benny fell "into a huge vat of bubbling toxic sludge" in their uncle Quack's lab. Uncle Quack tells the boys, "Maybe we won't tell your mom about this." The sludge gives Gordon superpowers. He makes a superhero suit and calls himself Kung Pow Chicken. His brother becomes Kung Pow Chicken's sidekick Egg Drop. The boys, who live in Fowladelphia, attend the Fowl Fall Festival with their classmates. One teacher warns the students, "No pecking or shoving, bok, bok, bok." When Gordon's tail feathers begin to wiggle, he knows evil is right around the corner.

Reading selection: Read chapter 3, "A Fowl Festival." All of the chickens lose their feathers with a loud POOF! Gordon and Benny run into a port-a-potty to change into their superhero costumes. Gordon gets a leotard wedgie. The duo learns that all of the chickens had eaten glowing cookies. They trace the cookies to Granny Goosebumps, the owner of a sweater booth. Kung Pow Chicken says, "My birdy senses are doing the Funky Chicken. That granny must be up to no good." When Granny Goosebumps traps Kung Pow Chicken in yarn, he frees himself and says, "I'm Kung Pow Chicken! You are doomed to go to jail!" The two get engaged in a "battle of knits." Granny Goosebumps manages to defeat Kung Pow Chicken and escapes. The chapter ends with our superhero saying, "I want to go home."

Read-alike recommendations: There are three more books in the series, all published in 2014. They are *Bok! Bok! Boom!*, *The Birdy Snatchers*, and *Heroes on the Side*. Sarah Dillard's *Extraordinary Warren: A Super Chicken* (Aladdin, 2014) is for a slightly younger audience and follows the story of a bespectacled chicken that gains superpowers. Its sequel is *Extraordinary Warren Saves the Day* (2014).

Solomons, David. *My Brother Is a Superhero*. Viking, 2015. Gr. 4–6.

First line: "My brother is a superhero and I could have been one too, except that I needed to go pee."

The pitch: Luke is pissed off. Sorry, poor choice of words. When Luke left the tree house to pee, his brother Zach gained superpowers. Apparently, the

tree house is situated at a junction between two universes. An alien named Zorban the Decider appeared and gave Zach superpowers because he was the first person Zorban saw. When Luke finds out, he is livid. He says, "That's not how you choose a savior of mankind. There has to at least be a prophecy written in an ancient book. This was like giving the Sword of Ultimate Power to a goldfish." Despite his anger, Luke helps his brother get a superhero name: Star Guy. Starman and Star Boy were already taken. Before he left, Zorban the Decider warned, "NEMESIS IS COMING."

Reading selection: Read the very end of chapter 3, "Star Guy," with the sentence: "After dinner, when I was supposed to be doing my homework on the computer, I decided to poke around on the Internet and see what I could find out about Nemesis." The chapter ends with Luke learning that Nemesis is a girl. Continue by reading all of chapter 4, "Hi-Mad Ork." Luke tells Zack that, as a superhero, he needs a secret phrase. He suggests "Hi-Mad Ork." Zack doesn't get it. Luke tells him to say it over and over. "Zack assumed the same pose. 'Hi-mad Ork . . . Hi-mad Ork . . .' As he repeated the phrase it became clear what he was actually saying. 'I'm a dork. . . . I'm a dork. . . . I'm a—' I couldn't hold a snigger in any longer." The chapter ends with the ominous sentence: "And instead of robots or aliens, there was something much more fearsome."

Read-alike recommendations: The sequel is *My Gym Teacher Is an Alien Overlord* (2016) where superpower-less Luke once again saves the day. *Captain Nobody* by Dean Pitchford (Putnam, 2009) also features a younger brother who doesn't have superpowers but still performs heroic deeds.

Trine, Greg. *Curse of the Bologna Sandwich* (Melvin Beederman, Superhero series). Holt, 2006. Gr. 3–4.

First line: "Melvin Beederman didn't feel like a superhero."

The pitch: Even though he finished at the top of his class at Superhero Academy, Melvin doesn't feel like a true superhero. He is unable to leap a building in a single bound. "It always took him five or six tries." He rarely uses his x-ray vision because it makes him uncomfortable seeing so much underwear. He does follow the Superhero Code: "Never say no to a cry for help" and heads to his assignment in Los Angeles, a city that has been without a superhero ever since Kareem Abdul-Jabbar retired. He teams up with a girl named Candace. She shares his superpowers—"She scored 500 points in a single basketball game. All dunks"—and the duo sets off to fight the McNasty brothers.

Reading selection: Read chapter 14, "The McNastys." All the McNastys smell bad. "Even their goldfish smelled bad. If you ever see extra bubbles in their fish tank, you'd better run and not look back." The two McNasty brothers, Filthy and Grunge, follow two rules. The first is: "Be nasty at all times." The second is: "Don't trust superheroes." While the McNastys are counting their loot—"If you withdraw cash from a bank, it's called money. If you steal it's called loot"—they get ready to face the new superhero in town. The chapter ends with the lines: "Filthy had a secret weapon. 'Melvin Beederman doesn't have a chance,' he said to himself."

Read-alike recommendations: Melvin returns in the following sequels: *The Revenge of the McNasty Brothers* (2006), *The Grateful Fred* (2006), *Terror in Tights* (2007), *The Fake Cape Caper* (2007), *Attack of the Valley Girls* (2008), *The Brotherhood of the Traveling Underpants* (2009), and *Invasion from Planet Dork* (2010).

Trine, Greg. *Dinos Are Forever* (Adventures of Jo Schmo series). Harcourt, 2012. Gr. 3–4.

First line: "Jo Schmo came from a long line of crime fighters."

The pitch: One day, Jo receives a mysterious package. She knows it is a mysterious package because the deliveryman says, "Mysterious package for Jo." Her second clue is written on the mysterious package itself. It reads, "Mysterious package: for Jo Schmo." Inside, she finds a red cape and a letter from her uncle Greg that says, "I am retiring from my life as a superhero and have enclosed my cape. Use it well." Jo seeks advice from her grandpa Joe, a retired sheriff. "'Who's there?' came a voice. 'It's Jo.' 'Joe?' 'No, Jo.' 'Oh, Jo. I thought I was talking to myself for a second there.'" Grandpa Joe tells granddaughter Jo that catching bad guys is a blast. When she puts on her cape, he says that she looks ready to save the world. Before she saves the world, however, she needs to learn about her new superpowers.

Reading selection: Read chapter 5, "Meanwhile, Back at the Jacuzzi." Grandpa Joe and Jo consult the Superhero Instruction Manual. To fly, she needs to think lofty thoughts. The flying lessons don't work so well, so they move on to stopping a train in its tracks. The manual says, "Stopping a train is all in the wrist." Jo is worried when she stands on the train tracks, but "before you could say 'Jo Schmo stopped the train,' Jo Schmo stopped the train. Just like that. It really was all in the wrist." The chapter ends with the line: "The train, of course, was completely demolished, but at least Jo Schmo wasn't."

Read-alike recommendations: The other books in the series are *Wyatt Burp Rides Again* (2012), *Shifty Business* (2013), and *Pinkbeard's Revenge* (2013). *Superheroes Don't Eat Veggie Burgers* by Gretchen Kelley (Holt, 2016) is a humorous adventure of a boy who makes up stories about a superhero named Dude Explodius. The stories all come true.

Urey, Gary. *Super Schnoz and the Gates of Smell.* Albert Whitman, 2013. Gr. 3–5.

First line: "My name is Andy Whiffler and I was born with a humongous honker."

The pitch: Andy's nose is so big "little people could use it for a sledding hill." He's teased a lot at school: "Hey, Honker Face" and "Andy the Big-Nosed Reindeer" are just two examples of the name-calling he endures. The teasing stops when his tormentors learn about his super sense of smell. Andy gives some boys the heads-up when he smells the scent of "black coffee, spearmint Lifesavers, garlic bagel with cream cheese, a hint of ripe body odor—Principal Cyrano." Andy's nose becomes a hit at school. He uses it to shield snoozing kids from their teachers and his sneeze is so loud it sets off the fire alarm, thus canceling a pop quiz. The kids play a new game at recess. Instead of hide-and-seek, they play hide-and-sniff. The students bring gross-smelling things from home for Andy to sniff out, things like "sandwich baggies full of fish guts, their dad's smelly socks, cat litter clumps, used diapers, moldy mac and cheese, rotten leftover egg salad, and dozens of other malodorous mixtures meant to offend mere mortals." And then, Andy learns about another superpower.

Reading selection: Read chapter 13, "It's a Bird . . . It's a Plane . . . It's Super Schnoz!" Andy's friends make him a superhero costume complete with an emblem of a nose with large nostrils on the shirt. Despite the fact that he chooses not to wear pointy black boots—"My old sneakers would be just fine"—Andy looks "Schnozalicious!" A gust of wind blasts through the backyard while Andy poses for a picture. The air inflates his nostrils "like two giant parachutes. My heart dropped into my stomach, my toes lifted off the ground, and my cape fluttered in the breeze. I was flying!"

Read-alike recommendations: Andy returns in the books *Super Schnoz and the Invasion of the Snore Snatchers* (2014) and *Super Schnoz and the Booger Blaster Breakdown* (2015).

CHAPTER 7

Mystery and Espionage

Kids love to help solve the mysteries along with the young (sometimes animal) heroes in this genre. Espionage stories, those that mostly follow James Bond–type boys and girls, often armed with extraordinary gadgets and resources, are closely related. They are also called "page-turners." Both types of books will keep reluctant readers quickly turning the pages to see what happens next.

Abbott, Tony. *The Crazy Case of Missing Thunder* (Goofballs series). Egmont USA, 2012. Gr. 3–4.

First line: "My name is Jeff Bunter, and I'm a Goofball."

The pitch: What Jeff means is that he's a Goofball private eye, a group he created with some friends. The origin of the name came about when Jeff was a one-year-old. He climbed down from his high chair with a bag of french fries and came back up with "four extra-long fries stuck in my nose and ears. I wiggled them all around." His father called him a Goofball. When Jeff found his

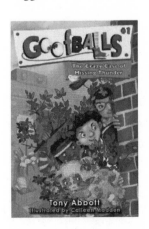

father's missing wallet later, his mother called him a Goofball private eye. Jeff teamed up with Brian, who was missing his pants when the two first met. The other members of the team are Mara and Kelly, two girls disguised with cheese and crackers on their faces. Over time, the four have solved the "Famous Riddle of the Exploding Rat Balloon" and the "Unbelievable Affair of the Totally Incredible Pizza Disaster." Now, they try to solve the mystery of a missing horse.

Reading selection: Read the entire chapter 4, "Rich, Rich, Rich!" The kids go to the home of the wealthy Randall Crandall to solve a mystery. They meet his butler Picksniff. When he tells the kids, "Walk this way," Jeff says they couldn't walk that way because "Picksniff had super-long legs, and we had to run to keep up with him." Keep reading into chapter 5, "The Sound of Thunder." Randall Crandall turns out to be a kid. Randall and Picksniff have a close relationship. Picksniff even completes Randall's sentences for him. Randall tells the Goofballs to pay attention and he demonstrates. "He squinched up his face as if he were going to sneeze. 'Ah-Ah-Ah-CHOO!' said Picksniff." End the selection when Randall tells the kids that his horse Thunder is missing.

Read-alike recommendations: The other titles in the series are *The Startling Story of the Stolen Statue* (2012), *Superhero Silliness* (2012), *The Mysterious Talent Show Mystery* (2013), *The Ha-Ha-Haunting of Hyde House* (2013), and *The Crazy Classroom Caper* (2014).

Black, Peter Jay. *Urban Outlaws*. Bloomsbury, 2014. Gr. 5–7.

First line: "Jack Fenton stood struck dumb, his eyes wide and staring, refusing to believe what he was looking at."

The pitch: Jack is a member of the Urban Outlaws, a gang of kids who live in a cool, secret bunker beneath London. The bunker even has a pinball machine. The Urban Outlaws' motto is: "Take only what others need." In other words, they "seized the financial assets of arms dealers, thugs, gangsters, and gave it to hospitals, charities, and caregivers." The old Robin Hood thing, stealing from the rich and giving to the poor. They also perform what they call "raking" or R.A.K.: Random Acts of Kindness, like leaving food and diapers for an impoverished young mother. Their mission eventually changes to saving the world from technology gone bad. Jack is concerned about suspicious behavior at a building under his surveillance. He calls for help from his fellow Urban Cowboys—Charlie, Slink, Obi, and little Wren.

Reading selection: Begin reading about two-thirds into chapter 3, beginning with the line: "Back in the main room, Jack and Charlie grabbed slices of cold pizza and gathered around Obi." They are watching the building with the changed locks on a screen. "Several trucks and vans had backed into the alleyway and it was a hive of activity." The kids notice a black SUV pull up. Out step two men and a woman, all wearing sunglasses at night. Jack explains that "CCTV face-recognition software doesn't work if you're wearing sunglasses. It recognizes facial patterns. Sunglasses screw that up." Despite Jack's protests, Charlie leaves to check out what's going on. She finds herself surrounded by the sunglass-wearing agents. One of them grabs her. He is "over six foot five and built like a tank." Another agent spots the camera on Charlie's shoulder. The chapter ends with the sentence: "The screen went blank."

Read-alike recommendations: Jack and the other Urban Outlaws continue to save the world in *Blackout* (2015), *Lockdown* (2015), and *Counterstrike* (2016). *The Infinity Code* by E. L. Young (Dial, 2007) is another book featuring young people using technology to help save the world. It is the first book in the S.T.O.R.M.

series. S.T.O.R.M. stands for Science and Technology to Over-Rule Misery. The companion books are *The Ghost Machine* (2007) and *The Black Sphere* (2009).

Butler, Dori Hillestad. *The Case of the Lost Boy* (Buddy Files series). Albert Whitman, 2010. Gr. 3–4.

First lines: "Hello! My name is King. I'm a dog. I'm also a detective."

The pitch: King finds himself in the dog pound, or as the dogs call it, the P-O-U-N-D. A basset hound explains, "We don't say it. We spell it." King makes a list to help solve the mystery of his missing owners, Kayla and her father. The first thing on the list is "Escape from the P-O-U-N-D." Instead, King is adopted by the new school principal and her son Connor. King is slightly outraged. "Humans do not adopt dogs. Dogs adopt humans!" Connor is not thrilled with his new home in Minnesota. He wants to return to California, where his father lives. Connor's mother gives King a new name—Buddy. Buddy is surprised to find himself back in his old neighborhood where Kayla lived. When Connor goes missing, Buddy enlists the help of his old friends, the neighborhood dogs, to locate his new owner.

Reading selection: Read chapter 6, "Smells like a Kidnapping." Buddy's friend Mouse reports that Connor is at the playground. When Buddy arrives, it turns out to be a false alarm. Several dogs report that they smell Connor. "Toast, cereal, soap, and sweaty socks, right?" Buddy has to tell them they have the wrong smell. "Connor smells like eggs, bacon, toothpaste, and dirt." We learn that sometimes dogs mix up information and "pretty soon the message is completely wrong." Two police officers show up at the playground and return Buddy back to Connor's mother. King thinks, "At least they aren't taking me back to the P-O-U-N-D." The two police officers say that a man tried to kidnap a kid in the same neighborhood just last week. The chapter ends with the lines: "Lost kids are usually found. But kidnapped kids? I don't want to think about it."

Read-alike recommendations: The other titles in the series are *The Case of the Mixed-Up Mutts* (2010), *The Case of the Missing Family* (2010), *The Case of the Fire Alarm* (2011), *The Case of the Library Monster* (2011), and *The Case of the School Ghost* (2012). The Fletcher Mystery series by Elizabeth Levy also features a dog sleuth. Fletcher is a basset hound who solves mysteries with the help of a flea. The titles are *A Hare-Raising Tale* (Aladdin, 2002), *The Principal on the Roof* (2002), *The Mixed-Up Mask Mystery* (2003), *The Mystery of Too Many Elvises* (2003), and *The Cool Ghoul Mystery* (2003).

Cronin, Doreen. *The Trouble with Chickens* (A J.J. Tully Mystery series). Balzer + Bray, 2011. Gr. 3–4.

First line: "It was a hot, sunny day when I met that crazy chicken."

The pitch: That crazy chicken's name is Millicent, but J.J. Tully calls her Moosh. J.J. Tully lives by Barb's country home after retiring as a search-and-rescue dog. Those in the profession "are a rare breed. We have to be half strength, half perseverance, and half obedience. Do your own math, tough guy—I'm making a point here." Moosh comes calling with her chicks, Dirt and Sugar. Moosh's other two chicks, Poppy and Sweetie, are missing. J.J. Tully takes the case for the payment of a cheeseburger. They find a ransom note that reads, "I have your peeps. It behooves you to rendezvous. Twilight. Your place." The trail leads J.J. Tully to the country house where he finds Vince, "thirty-seven pounds of shiny brown mutt. He had a long, skinny build, beady eyes, and a giant white funnel around his neck. He looked like a cross between a dachshund and a lamp." The rumor is that Vince is "a little off his rocker."

Reading selection: Read the very short chapter 10, "Funnel Vision." The narration has shifted from J.J. Tully's to Vince's. He obviously dislikes "J.J. the Hero Dog." He gloats that he is luring J.J. Tully into a trap. "But Hero Dog isn't like Barb's usual rejects—the orphan baby birds, the mangy stray cats. I'll have to figure out his weak spot when I have him up close and personal." Vince calls himself the alpha dog who doesn't like company. As he leaps off the table in front of the window, his funnel catches the edge of a lamp and breaks it. It's the first time we realize that Vince has kidnapped Poppy and Sweetie. The chapter ends with the lines: "Two tiny chickens squawked. I couldn't have planned it better myself."

Read-alike recommendations: The sequel is titled *The Legend of Diamond Lil* (2012). The chicks star in their own Chicken Squad series beginning with *Chicken Squad: The First Misadventure* (Atheneum, 2014). The other titles include *The Case of the Weird Blue Chicken: The Next Misadventure* (2014), and *Into the Wild: Yet Another Misadventure* (2016). The Platypus Police Squad series by Jarrett Krosoczka is another mystery featuring talking animals. The books in this series include *The Frog Who Croaked* (Walden Pond, 2013), *The Ostrich Conspiracy* (2014), *Last Panda Standing* (2015), and *Never Say Narwhal* (2015).

Gibbs, Stuart. *Belly Up* (FunJungle series). Simon & Schuster, 2010. Gr. 4–7.

First line: "I'd just been busted for giving the chimpanzees water balloons when I first heard something was wrong at Hippo River."

The pitch: Teddy, a twelve-year-old whose parents work at the FunJungle theme park and zoo, gets into trouble with the park's security officers after he tried to help the animals. Tourists pelted the chimpanzees for fun. One said, "I'll bet I can hit him right in the head" The chimps retaliated by throwing water balloons at the tourists. Security catches up with Teddy and he tells them, "If I hadn't given the chimps water balloons, they'd have thrown *poop*." Henry the Hippo, the park's mascot, turns up dead in his exhibit. The public doesn't know that Henry was the meanest animal in the zoo. Teddy is convinced that Henry was murdered and sets off to solve the mystery of his demise. In doing so, Teddy becomes a target. He receives a text directing him to go to the World of Reptiles exhibit after the tourists have gone home.

Reading selection: Read a section of chapter 8, "Black Mamba," beginning with the long sentence: "FunJungle had more poisonous snakes than any other zoo in the world: cobras, death adders, kraits, asps, coral snakes, cottonmouths, gaboon vipers, fer-de-lances, copperheads, taipans, bandy-bandys, bushmasters, sidewinders, two dozen kinds of rattlesnakes, and a huge aquarium filled with sea snakes, which were fascinating to watch." FunJungle has one more poisonous snake, the black mamba. "They've killed more people than any other kind of snake." Teddy notices a small gap in the glass from the black mamba case. End the selection with the line: "Something hissed behind me."

Read-alike recommendations: The other titles in the series include *Poached* (2014), *Big Game* (2015), and *Panda-monium* (2017).

Gibbs, Stuart. *Spy School.* Simon & Schuster, 2012. Gr. 4–7.

First lines: "'Hello, Ben,' said the man in my living room. 'My name is Alexander Hale. I work for the CIA.' And just like that, my life became interesting."

The pitch: The CIA has had its eye on twelve-year-old Ben for some time, mostly because Ben has accessed their website 728 times. They noticed other things like when "you spiked Dirk Dennett's Pepsi with Ex-Lax—and frankly, that kid was asking for it." One reason the CIA tells Ben they like him for their school is that he has Level 16 math skills. "I thought *everyone* could do complex mathematical equations in their heads . . . or instantly calibrate how many days, weeks, or minutes they'd been alive. I was 3,832 days old when I found out otherwise." Alexander Hale whisks Ben to the Academy of Espionage.

Reading selection: Read the last half of chapter 2, beginning with the line: "'What's wrong?' I asked." Alexander Hale notices something is amiss at the academy. He tells Ben to run for the front doors. "Something cracked in the distance. A tiny explosion erupted in the snow to my left. Someone was shooting at me!" Once inside the school, Ben is knocked down by a girl we later learn is the daughter of Alexander Hale. She informs Ben that there has been a security breach and by her count, they are surrounded by forty-one "professional, heavily armed, and extremely dangerous" enemy operatives. The chapter ends with the sentence: "Welcome to spy school."

Read-alike recommendations: The sequels include *Spy Camp* (2013), *Evil Spy School* (2015), and *Spy Ski School* (2016). *Playing with Fire* by Bruce Hale (Hyperion, 2013) features an orphan who is sent to a spy training school disguised as an orphanage. Its sequels are *Thicker Than Water* (2014) and *Ends of the Earth* (2015).

Keane, Dave. *The Haunted Toolshed* **(Joe Sherlock, Kid Detective series). HarperCollins, 2006. Gr. 3–4.**

First lines: "My name is Joe Sherlock. But almost everybody just calls me Sherlock. Never Joe."

The pitch: Joe is a big fan of the legendary Sherlock Holmes. He's seen just about every detective movie ever made, from the good ones to "the old black-and-white ones where everybody stands around talking so much that you wake up on the floor two hours later in a pool of your own drool." Joe's very first job is Case #000001—The Case of the Haunted Toolshed, a case that makes Joe "feel like I have a pair of live squirrels in my stomach and two corks shoved up my nostrils."

Reading selection: Read chapter 3, "Strange Goings-On." A neighbor, Mr. Asher, wants to hire Joe to solve his problem. "'I may have . . . a poltergeist.' 'I see,' I say like any thoughtful detective would say, although I'm really thinking that I have absolutely no idea what 'poltergeist' means." Joe learns that it means a kind of ghost. Mr. Asher is worried that the ghost is giving his mother "a terrible case of flatulence." Again, Joe has no clue what "flatulence" means. His little sister Hailey explains, "That means she's farting up a storm." While Mr. Asher is giving more details about the case, they all hear a "hollow, spine-straightening moan from another world." The chapter ends with Joe thinking, "The evil spirits from beyond this life have followed Mr. Asher down the street from his house! The poltergeist is now in my house!"

Read-alike recommendations: The other titles in the series are *The Neighborhood Stink* (2006), *The Missing Monkey-Eye Diamond* (2006), *The Headless Mummy* (2007), and *The Art Teacher's Vanishing Masterpiece* (2007). *Sherlock Sam and the Missing Heirloom in Katong* by A. J. Low (Andrews McMeel, 2016) is another book featuring a Sherlock Holmes fan. Its companion book is *Sherlock Sam and the Ghostly Moans in Fort Canning* (2016).

Kehret, Peg. *Stolen Children.* **Dutton, 2008. Gr. 5–7.**

First line: "Amy's babysitting course taught her basic first aid, bedtime tips, and how to change a diaper, but it did not cover what to do if two thugs with a gun showed up."

The pitch: The incident with two thugs with a gun happened on Amy's very first day babysitting three-year-old Kendra, the daughter of a fairly wealthy family. Fourteen-year-old Amy is trying to deal with the hit-and-run death of her father. She feels responsible because they argued before he died. His last words to her were, "I'm ashamed of you." She takes a new babysitting job for the Edgerton family when their regular nanny is unavailable. While Kendra is napping, Amy hears a sudden noise. When she checks on Kendra, the little girl is not in her bed. Amy regrets leaving the outside doors unlocked. She has the awful feeling that someone has kidnapped Kendra.

Reading selection: Read chapter 3. Amy is trying to decide if she should call the police or Kendra's mother first. She hears a vehicle in the driveway and sees a tall man. She tells him she needs help when another man shouts, "Stop her!" Amy notices Kendra in the van. Amy runs into the house, but one of the men gets in and points a gun at her. They realize they need to kidnap both girls now. As they drive away, Amy overhears their plan. "Now two families will be desperate to get their kid back." The men also reveal that Kendra's regular nanny was supposed to be in on the plan but that she split. The men threaten to kill the nanny if she tells anyone of the kidnapping. The chapter ends with Amy reacting to what they just said. "A chill crept down the back of her neck. She and Kendra had been kidnapped by a man who was capable of murder."

Read-alike recommendation: Author Kehret wrote another kidnapping story for young readers titled *Abduction!* (Dutton, 2004), the story of thirteen-year-old Bonnie whose kindergarten-age brother got into a stranger's car.

Korman, Gordon. *Swindle.* Scholastic, 2008. Gr. 4–7.

First line: "SNEAKING OUT AT NIGHT—HELPFUL HINTS: (i) When lying to your parents, maintain EYE CONTACT!"

The pitch: Griffin lies to his parents about going to a sleepover at a friend's house. He's really hanging out at a supposedly haunted house scheduled for demolition the very next day. During the night, Griffin finds a Babe Ruth baseball card in an old-fashioned desk. In the morning, the boys barely escape before a wrecking ball shatters the house. Griffin takes the card to Palomino's Emporium where the owner buys it for $125. Griffin learns afterward that he has been swindled. The card is worth one million dollars. He is determined to get the card back, even if it means breaking into Palomino's Emporium and stealing it. Griffin enlists a group of kids by sending out notes that begin with the line: "You have been chosen for your special skills."

Reading selection: Read the checklist at the end of chapter 6. Griffin lists his plan of attack for the Great Baseball Card Heist. Read the very short chapter 7. He left one major obstacle off the list: the guard dog, a very mean Doberman named Luther. Continue reading the first part of chapter 8, where Griffin and his friend Ben enlist the help of animal lover Savannah. She tries her best to befriend Luther. Savannah tosses a toy poodle over the fence to "bring out the playful side of his personality." The toy never reaches the ground. The dog rips it apart. "And there stood the Doberman at the center of a scattering of pink rubber shreds. The scene looked like someone had fed a box of erasers

through a jet engine." Savannah says that Luther is a magnificent animal. End the reading with the line: "*Magnificent* was not the word Griffin and Ben would have chosen."

Read-alike recommendations: Griffin and his friends have more adventures in the following sequels: *Zoobreak* (2009), *Framed* (2010), *Showoff* (2012), *Hideout* (2013), *Jackpot* (2014), and *Unleashed* (2015).

O'Donnell, Liam. *The Case of the Slime Stampede* (Tank & Fizz series). Orca, 2015. Gr. 3–5.

First line: "The principal's car got eaten first."

The pitch: Green slime not only covers the principal's car but it also slurps the playground at Gravelmuck Elementary. Fizz is a fourth-grade detective. And he's a goblin. He asks the reader, "You don't have anything against goblins, do you?" Fizz's best friend is a troll named Tank. Tank is a girl who loves gadgets. Both Fizz and Tank love solving mysteries. They need to find out how their school caretaker's (Mr. Snag, who is an ogre by the way) slimes got loose. Their investigation leads them to check the school's locks with Tank's special equipment. "From sonic hatchdrivers to pocket-sized spectroscopic enhancers, Tank is the troll with the tools." They soon find themselves in trouble with Principal Weaver, a spider.

Reading selection: Read chapter 7, "New Caretakers and Deal Makers." The chapter opens with Weaver saying, "Look who wandered into my web." Dark shapes skitter all around while Weaver talks to Fizz and Tank. "Weaver's spider babies lurked. Hundreds of them, scurrying through the school. Watching and reporting back to Mommy. The whole room was alive with them. Alive and hungry." Weaver warns them to stop their investigation. Before they leave her office, the new caretaker, Mr. Zallin, walks in. Tank is fascinated by the gizmos on his tool belt. She's almost hypnotized by them. The chapter ends with Fizz worrying. "This was bad. First I'd lost our school caretaker. Was I losing my detective partner too?"

Read-alike recommendations: The second book in the series is *The Case of the Battling Bots* (2016). The Chet Gecko Mystery series by Bruce Hale also features an unusual detective. In this case, a gecko. The titles are *The Chameleon Wore Chartreuse* (Harcourt, 2001), *The Mystery of Mr. Nice* (2001), *Farewell, My Lunchbag* (2001), *The Big Nap* (2001), *The Hamster of the Baskervilles* (2002), *This Gum for Hire* (2002), *The Malted Falcon* (2003), *Trouble Is My Beeswax* (2004), *Give My Regrets to Broadway* (2004), *Murder, My Tweet* (2004), *The Possum Always Rings Twice* (2006), *Key Lardo* (2006), *Hiss Me Deadly* (2007), *From Russia with Lunch* (2009), and *Dial M for Mongoose* (2009).

CHAPTER 8

Outdoor Survival

Gary Paulsen's Brian series that started with the book *Hatchet* is often credited for the popularity of this genre. Young characters often find themselves in danger from the elements. Readers find themselves surviving alongside the characters in their imaginations, wondering if they, too, could survive the conditions.

Bancks, Tristan. *On the Run*. Margaret Ferguson, 2015. Gr. 5–7.

First line: "'You keep runnin', you'll only go to jail tired,' Ben Silver muttered."

The pitch: Ben is making a stop-motion detective/zombie movie in his home in Australia when there's a heavy knock at the door. "Hello. Police!" Four officers want to talk to Ben's parents, who are not at home. Ben asks if they want to leave a message, and one officer says, "No, we'll catch up to them." No sooner do they leave than Ben's parents race up and make Ben and his little sister Olive jump into the car. Ben cannot get a clear explanation from his parents about their actions, only that the family is going on a vacation. Ben is surprised to hear that. They weren't really one of those "family-movie-night, camp-in-the-backyard, let's-discuss-this-and-get-everyone's-opinion kind of families. They were more of a dinner-in-front-of-the-TV, key's-under-the-mat, if-you-want-breakfast-make-it-yourself kind of family." His father drives to an old cabin in the woods that belongs to Ben's grandfather. He's trying to figure out his parents' strange behavior and eventually concludes that they are on the run from the law.

Reading selection: Read the chapter titled "Flesh and Blood." It's nighttime. Ben wakes up his parents and sister and tells them that he saw police officers in the woods. The four of them crawl through a hole in the floor and make it outside. "An explosive crash came from inside the cabin. A light went on, a moving light. A bright flashlight. Shouting, several voices at once, the kind of raid that Ben had seen on TV." Ben's father has left behind a bag of money. Ben wrestles with his conscience. "Would he turn them in, run, or follow his parents who had done a very bad thing?" He grabs the money and runs with his sister. In pursuit, the police cut them off from their parents. Ben falls. The chapter ends with the line: "His head hit something hard and there was a bright white flash that stopped everything."

Read-alike recommendation: Hide and Seek by Katy Grant (Peachtree, 2010) is the story of Chase, a geocacher who finds two boys at a campground. He learns they have been kidnapped by their father.

Brown, Peter. *Wild Robot*. Little, Brown, 2016. Gr. 3–6.

First lines: "Our story begins on the ocean, with wind and rain and thunder and lightning and waves. A hurricane roared and raged through the night. And in the middle of the chaos, a cargo ship was sinking. . . ."

The pitch: When one thinks of the wilderness, trees, bears, and the like often come to mind. Not robots. This is a wilderness story, but instead of a kid like Brian in the Hatchet books, it features a robot. A robot named Roz. When the boat carrying Roz and several other robots sinks, her crate washes ashore on an island. The animals that live on the island fear Roz. They think she's a monster. There are no humans to help if something goes wrong. Roz learns to survive in the wilderness on her own.

Reading selection: Read chapters 8–13. They are all very short. In chapter 8, "The Pinecones," Roz seeks shelter after being pelted by pinecones falling from the trees. Continue with chapter 9, "The Mountain." Roz climbs a mountain, looks around, and for the first time realizes she is stranded on an island. Chapter 10, "The Reminder," is one paragraph in length. Roz decides the island is her home. Chapter 11, "The Robot Sleeps," is one page in length and shows the "first night of the robot's life." Chapter 12, "The Storm," finds Roz getting caught in a mudslide. She manages to grab onto a tree. "The robot locked her arms and legs around the tree and waited for the storm to blow over." Chapter 13, "The Aftermath," finds Roz discovering a hole in the side of the mountain, a safe place for a robot now covered in dents and scratches. The selection ends with the line: "She stomped across the hillside and up to the cave, but never stopped to wonder what might be lurking within."

Read-alike recommendations: The 8th Continent by Matt London (Razorbill, 2014) is another book featuring a robot on the ocean. The robot helps two kids try to transform "The Pacific Garbage Patch" into a continent. Its sequels include *Welcome to the Jungle* (2015), *Born to Be Wild* (2015), and *We Built This City* (2016).

D'Ath, Justin. *Crocodile Attack* (Extreme Adventures series). Kane Miller, 2010. Gr. 3–5.

First line: "Black ski cap, dark blue raincoat, wet leather boots."

The pitch: That's a brief description of the man who kidnaps Sam and his two-year-old cousin Nissa. The man is robbing a store when the cyclone siren goes off. He panics, thinking he hears a police siren, and grabs Nissa. Sam runs after them and is forced into a pickup truck. The kidnapper speeds past a sign that reads: "DRY SEASON ROAD ONLY" and another sign that says: "CAUTION FLOODWAY." Suddenly, "a wide brown wave of water rolled across the hood and up over the windshield. Day turned into night." The truck enters the Crocodile River and heads downstream toward the ocean. Sam is sure his life is over. But that's not the worst. A snake bites Sam, Nissa goes overboard, and the kidnapper is injured. Sam and Nissa finally make it to a small island only to find a wild boar stranded there with them. Sam arms himself with an animal bone. He hears a splash and looks into the darkness. "There was no sign of the boar."

Reading selection: Read chapter 19, "Yizards." Dawn is approaching. Sam ponders their situation. "I remembered how the wild boar had disappeared, and my skin prickled. Deep down I suspected what might have happened, but I didn't want to think about it." Nissa says, "Yizard," and Sam sees a baby crocodile. Worried the little creature is calling its mother, Sam lifts it by its tail and tosses it into the water. Nissa happily announces, "Nother yizard," and Sam realizes their little island is basically one large crocodile's nest. Nissa next says, "Big yizard." The chapter ends with the following passage: "That thirteen-foot crocodile swimming towards us *wasn't* a computer-generated special effect. It was real. 'Stay behind me,' I said to Nissa, and picked up the buffalo bone."

Read-alike recommendations: The other titles in the series include *Bushfire Rescue* (2010), *Shark Bait* (2010), *Scorpion Sting* (2010), *Spider Bite* (2011), *Man-Eater* (2011), *Killer Whale* (2015), and *Grizzly Trap* (2015).

Gutman, Dan. *Getting Air.* Simon & Schuster, 2007. Gr. 4–7.

First line: "This is my ultimate fantasy."

The pitch: Jimmy's fantasy is to complete the first ever 1080 on his skateboard at the X Games with his supermodel girlfriend looking on. Jimmy's reality is that his skateboard falls out of the airplane's over-head bin and hits him on the head. Jimmy, his sister Julia, and his two skateboarding buddies Henry and David are flying to California to attend the X Games. The airplane is taken over by four hijackers. Jimmy manages to knock out one of the hijackers with his skateboard. Passengers overtake the other three hijackers. Jimmy and his friends check on the condition of the pilot and the copilot.

Reading selection: Read chapter 6, "Final Approach." The pilot and copilot are both dead. The radio is busted. No one on the airplane knows how to fly. Henry has taken a few flying lessons on small aircraft, but he still freaks out. "I know there's an electrical system, fuel system, fire-detection system, hydraulic system, cabin-pressurization system. But I don't know how to work them!" The engines stop working. Henry tries unsuccessfully to steer between trees. Jimmy knows that they all should probably leave the cockpit but says, "We couldn't stop looking at the trees coming at us. It was hypnotizing. We were frozen." The chapter ends with the line: "And that was the last thing I remembered."

Read-alike recommendation: The graphic novel *Wild Ride: A Graphic Guide Adventure*, written by Liam O'Donnell and illustrated by Mike Deas (Orca, 2007), features three kids and an adult who survive a plane crash in the wilderness. The adult turns murderous and the kids have to deal not only with him but also a forest fire and a grizzly bear.

Johnson, Terry Lynn. *Ice Dogs.* **Houghton Mifflin Harcourt, 2014. Gr. 4–7.**
First line: "All eight of my dogs are stretched in front of me in pairs along the gangline."

The pitch: Victoria's Alaskan dogsled team collides into a parked Corvette and she finds "a weight in the sled bag—a side mirror. Glancing to see if anyone noticed, I grab it and nonchalantly toss it away." Later on, while on a thirty-five-mile dogsled run, Victoria finds herself in bigger trouble. She realizes, "There's snow on the way and I forgot to check the forecast before I left. Crap." Victoria finds an unconscious boy her age who had wrapped his snowmobile around a birch tree. The boy, Chris, is bleeding from a head wound. He directs Victoria to where he thinks his house is located. Victoria, Chris, and the dogs go in the wrong direction—into a blizzard.

Reading selection: Read the middle portion of chapter 15, beginning with the sentences: "I turn to start moving again just as I hear a different kind of scream—high-pitched and distinctly girly. It's Chris." A huge cow moose charges the sled. Victoria manages to throw a snowshoe at the moose, causing it to turn and run back down the trail. Unfortunately, the dogs, tied to the sled, run after it. Victoria grabs the gangline and is dragged on the ground, leaving Chris behind. The dogs "are trained to run straight down a trail" and won't turn around. After bouncing up and down the trail for some time, Victoria loses her grip and is run over by the sled. Finish by reading the following passage: "I look up just in time to see the sled disappear around the next bend. Shakily, I sit up. I've lost my hat and snow is packed solidly up my sleeves, down my neck, up my nose. I'm starving. Alone in the winter bush. Wet. And I've lost my dog team."

Read-alike recommendation: *Ice Island* by Sherry Shahan (Delacorte. 2012) features a girl named Tatum who is out on a dogsled run with a boy named Cole. They run into an Alaskan blizzard.

Key, Watt. *Terror at Bottle Creek.* **Farrar Straus Giroux, 2016. Gr. 5–7.**

First line: "Dad said it was too early to be worried about the hurricane."

The pitch: Despite his father's confidence, thirteen-year-old Cort is not so sure about the approaching hurricane. The television reports that it is on its way to the Alabama coast where they live. "And with a name like Igor, it sounded cruel and deadly." The hurricane arrives when Cort is alone with two neighbor girls, Liza and Francie. No adults around. The kids find themselves in the middle of the swamp, surrounded by spiders, bears, wild boars, alligators, and cottonmouth snakes.

Reading selection: Read the short chapter 29. The kids are huddled in a tree at 4:00 a.m., waiting out the hurricane. Suddenly, Liza yelps. "I waved the light over her leg and saw the cottonmouth hanging and whipping from her heel." Cort knocks the snake loose and starts swearing. Cort inspects Liza's heel and sees "two fang marks, oozing something milky and bloody." He makes a cut from some glass shrapnel and starts sucking the venom out. The chapter ends with Liza asking what's going to happen to her. "'I don't know.' 'Yes, you do, Cort. You know about this.' She was right. I did. But I wished I didn't."

Read-alike recommendation: Alabama Moon (2006), also by author Key, features another wilderness-savvy boy who uses his survival skills to elude folks who want to put him in a boys' home.

Korman, Gordon. *Chasing the Falconers* **(On the Run series). Scholastic, 2005. Gr. 4–7.**

First line: "It wasn't a prison."

The pitch: It looked like a farm. It didn't have "bars, cells, electrified fencing, guard towers, or razor wire." But make no mistake, it wasn't a luxury hotel. "Welcome to Alcatraz Junior," also known as Sunnydale Farm, where juvenile offenders are sent. Eighteen boys and twelve girls have little free time: seven hours of school, twenty minutes of "Gulp 'n' Gag" lunch, and the rest of the time, starting at 5:00 a.m., "tilling, planting, fertilizing, pruning, and picking. They tended the chickens and fought with the geese. And they milked the cows." Fifteen-year-old Aiden Falconer and his eleven-year-old sister Meg are in Sunnydale because there was nowhere else to go after their parents were sent to federal prison. The Falconers, both criminologists, were approached by an undercover CIA operative, Agent Frank Lindenauer, to help with the war on terror. Instead, they were both arrested for "aiding the enemies of their country." Agent Lindenauer, the only man who could help them, "had disappeared off the face of the earth." Aiden is working in the chicken coop when he accidentally starts a fire. It reaches the barn and then the dormitories.

Reading selection: Start reading halfway into chapter 3, with the sentence: "The girls' dormitory was smaller than the boys', but with identical rows of bunk beds on each side of the room." Meg is the only girl in the dorm when the "ceiling disinte-grated, and it was raining fire." She tries to smash a window but it is security glass "with wire mesh embedded in each pane." Aiden runs in through the fire wrapped in a blanket. He grabs two more blankets and soaks them in the shower. The sib-lings burst through the opening and encounter "extreme heat, and, most terrifying of all, a total absence of air—a baking vacuum." Once outside, Meg convinces her brother that they need to leave Sunnydale in order to help prove their parents' in-nocence. The chapter ends with the sentence: "They sprinted for the cornfield."

Read-alike recommendations: Aiden and Meg's story continues in *Fugitive Factor* (2005), *Now You See Them, Now You Don't* (2005), *The Stowaway Solu-tion* (2005), *Public Enemies* (2005), and *Hunting the Hunter* (2006). Meg and Aiden are also featured in Korman's Kidnapped trilogy. Those titles are *The Abduction* (Scholastic, 2006), *The Search* (2006), and *The Rescue* (2006).

Monninger, Joseph. *Crash* **(Stay Alive series). Scholastic, 2014. Gr. 4–7.**

First lines: "Survival Tip #1. Whenever you are lost, follow any body of water downstream."

The pitch: Remember that survival tip. Stick to the water. Towns and cit-ies are often built around water. "Civilization means help and rescue." A plane carrying the crew for a teen-based television magazine show goes down in the Alaskan wilderness. The pilot does his best to aim the plane for a lake. "He did not see the branch that came through the window and ended his days at the cockpit." Another passenger dies in the crash and another is critically hurt. Two adults, one dog—the show's mascot Buford—and six teens climb out of the wreckage. Luckily, they had landed in ten feet of water and not too far from shore. One of the teens, Paul, is the first off the plane. "He put his head back up and looked around. Mountains, water, trees. That was all he saw."

Reading selection: Read a little more than halfway into chapter 3, beginning with "E knew what they needed to do from camping trips with her parents, but

she couldn't get anyone's attention." The singing star makes a high-pitched scream her brother calls the Hippo Hurricane. Once the other survivors quiet down and look at her, she directs them to build a fire. "'What was that sound?' someone asked, but at least people began moving." They get a fire started on the beach. The girl, known as E, is filled with pride. The chapter ends with the following line: "It threw light when it grew to knee height and she saw people's outlines slowly emerge from the darkness: the survivors, the ones who had come flying like an arrow from the sky."

Read-alike recommendations: Author Monninger has three more titles in the series: *Cave-In* (2014), the story of kids on a field trip who try to survive an earthquake, *Breakdown* (2014), featuring summer camp kids stranded miles from anywhere, and *Flood* (2014), a story of kids stranded by flood-waters.

Tarshis, Lauren. *Five Epic Disasters* **(I Survived True Stories series). Scholastic, 2014. Gr. 4–6.**

First line: "January 12, 1888, dawned bright and sunny in Groton, Dakota Territory, a tiny town on America's enormous wind-swept prairie."

The pitch: Kids all over the area head to school without their winter coats and boots. They have been trapped in their homes for weeks, kept indoors by frigid temperatures that plunged to forty degrees below zero. And now the temperature is around twenty degrees, comparatively balmy. Not all the parents trust the extreme temperature shift, and they keep their kids at home. They were smart. This is one of five disasters covered in this book. The others feature the sinking of the *Titanic* in 1912, the great Boston molasses flood of 1919, and more recently, the Japanese tsunami of 2011 and the Henryville tornado of 2012. Author Tarshis is known to her friends as "the disaster queen." The opening story is one she calls "The Children's Blizzard, 1888."

Reading selection: Read the section of chapter 1, titled "An Explosion." The children in the school hear a loud roaring sound, and the building is soon pounded by snow and sleet. The local townsfolk work quickly to evacuate the children. The teachers count every child. Continue reading the next section, titled "Swallowed by Darkness." The adults miss young Walter, who runs back into school to retrieve his prized possession, a perfume bottle. When he runs back outside, the procession has already gone. Walter is stuck outside in a blizzard. The passage ends with the following: "He realized that nobody knew that he wasn't on the sleds, huddled among classmates, heading for home. It was as though he had tumbled off Earth and into space—a frozen, swirling darkness."

Read-alike recommendations: A second collection of tales in the series is *Nature Attacks* (2015). There are several titles in the author's companion I Survived series. These include *The Sinking of the* Titanic, *1912* (2010), *The Shark Attacks of 1916* (2010), *Hurricane Katrina, 2005* (2011), *The Bombing of Pearl Harbor, 1941* (2011), *The San Francisco Earthquake, 1906* (2012), *The Attacks of September 11, 2001* (2012), *The Battle of Gettysburg, 1863* (2013), *The Japanese Tsunami, 2011* (2013), *The Nazi Invasion, 1944* (2014), *The Destruction of Pompeii, AD 79* (2014), *The Great Chicago Fire, 1871* (2015), *The Joplin Tornado, 2011* (2015), *The* Hindenburg *Disaster, 1937* (2016), and *The Eruption of Mount St. Helens, 1980* (2016).

CHAPTER 9

Animals

.

Kids love animals. They always have and they always will. This collection of titles includes fantasy animals and more realistic fiction animals, as well as nonfiction animal books. A few animal picture books are even included for upper elementary reluctant readers.

Applegate, Katherine. *The One and Only Ivan*. Harper, 2012. Gr. 3–6.
First lines: "I am Ivan. I am a gorilla. It's not as easy as it looks."
The pitch: Ivan is known as the "Freeway Gorilla. The Ape at Exit 8. The One and Only Ivan. Mighty Silverback." He used to be wild, but he was captured by humans when he was little. Ivan was sold to Mack, who owns the Exit 8 Big Top Mall and Video Arcade. He is on display with other animals including an elephant named Stella. There is also a homeless dog named Bob who sneaks in and out of the little zoo. Few people stop by the mall these days, so Mack buys a baby elephant named Ruby to drum up business. As Stella dies, she makes Ivan promise that Ruby won't have the same fate she did, living her life in cramped quarters. Ivan makes that promise but has no clue how to make it work. While he sets out to make a plan, he remembers what it was like when he first came to live with Mack.
Reading selection: Read the short chapter titled "The Temporary Human." When Ivan was little, he lived with Mack and his wife, Helen, in their home. Ivan broke a lot of things, including a blender, and he says, "I squeezed two tubes of toothpaste and a bottle of glue into it." The couple even took Ivan to a restaurant where Mack would jokingly say, "Could I have some extra ketchup for my kid?" Continue reading the next chapters "Hunger" and "Still Life." Helen brings home a painting of fruit in a bowl. She says that Ivan likes it. Mack disagrees and says, "Ivan likes to roll up poop and throw it at squirrels." Ivan is inspired to make art and scoops frosting off Helen's chocolate cake and smears

it on the refrigerator door. Finish the reading with the chapter titled "Punishment." Here it is in its entirety: "I soon learned that humans can screech even louder than monkeys. After that, I was never allowed in the kitchen."

Read-alike recommendation: Chained by Lynne Kelly (Farrar Straus Giroux, 2012) is the moving story of an imprisoned circus elephant.

Barr, Brady. *Scrapes with Snakes! True Stories of Adventures with Animals* **(National Geographic Kids Chapters series). National Geographic, 2015. Gr. 3–6.**

First lines: "I was waist-deep in water in a muddy swamp. I was trying not to think about the leeches that might be crawling up my legs."

The pitch: Zoologist Brady Barr's favorite animals are reptiles. Not only does he find himself in a leech-infested swamp to chase large reptiles, but he also enters rivers, walks into bat-poop-filled caves, and sends robots down into aardvark holes. While wading in this particular river in India, he and his partner Gerry learn about a snake the locals believe is eating their cows. As Barr wades into the dark water in search of this snake, all he can think about is "a snake big enough to swallow a cow could certainly swallow a man!"

Reading selection: Read the second half of chapter 2, "Swamp Slog," starting with the line: "Gerry and I searched for a long time without seeing anything." After they catch a few small snakes and pick leeches off their legs, the two men are ready to call it quits. "We were both thinking this giant snake story was simply that: a tall tale." A ten-year-old boy named Ramkrishna has been watching them. He tells the men that they are looking in the wrong spot. Read the next chapter, "Wrestling a Giant." Brady and Gerry grab a huge snake, but "as soon as my hands touched that snake, I knew that we were in big trouble." The snake gets its coils around both men and throws them around in the water. Ramkrishna runs for help. The chapter ends with the snake looping a coil around Brady's neck. He says, "Within seconds I could barely breathe. I became light-headed, and I was close to passing out. The battle seemed to go on forever."

Read-alike recommendations: Author Barr's companion book is *Crocodile Encounters! And More True Stories of Adventures with Animals* (2012). Select recommendations from the National Geographic Kids Chapters series include *Dog Finds Lost Dolphins! And More True Stories of Amazing Animal Heroes* by Elizabeth Carney (2012) and *Kangaroos to the Rescue! And More True Stories of Amazing Animal Heroes* by Moira Rose Donohue (2015).

Bauer, Michael Gerard. *Just a Dog.* **Scholastic, 2010. Gr. 4–6.**

First line: "The day my dad said Mister Mosely was 'just a dog,' my mum punched him."

The pitch: For the most part, Corey agrees with his dad that Mister Mosely is just a dog, an ordinary dog. Mister Mosely "didn't have any special superpowers and he didn't go around rescuing people or catching bad guys the way that police dog on TV does." Mister Mosely is a tall Dalmatian mix who is "mostly white." When little Corey saw him for the first time in a litter of pups, he wanted the one that was "mostly white." However, he couldn't quite say the word "mostly." It came out "mosely" and that is how Mister Mosely got his name. That's just one of the stories Corey shares with us. Many of the stories are very funny. Like the time his little sister Amelia got a marker pen and drew round glasses, bushy eyebrows, a mustache, and spiky hair on Mister Mosely. Corey's mother "laughed so much, one time I think I heard her make a little fart noise, and I didn't think Mum even did that kind of stuff." Of the stories Corey shares, he says, "And they will all be true. Even the ones that I wish weren't."

Reading selection: Read chapter 16, "My Favorite Mister Mosely Story." Mister Mosely always waited for Corey to come home from school. His tail would start wagging "and then he'd start dancing around in a bit of a circle because our house was way down at the end of the street and he wouldn't be sure if it was really me or not." Corey starts playing a game where he'd change his appearance and the way he walked to see if he could confuse Mister Mosely. Corey's laugh always gave himself away. Continue reading the short chapter 17, "Mister Mosely and the Stupid Trick." One day coming home from school, Corey wears a mask he made in art class. "It looked a bit like the Joker from *Batman*, only better and scarier and with a lot more colors in it." He scares Mister Mosely by growling while wearing the mask. The chapter ends with the sober line: "I was still laughing when the car hit him."

Read-alike recommendation: When Friendship Followed Me Home by Paul Griffin (Dial, 2016) is another moving dog story with moments of levity. Ben rescues an abandoned dog named Flip from an alley.

Boelts, Maribeth. *The PS Brothers.* Houghton Mifflin Harcourt, 2010. Gr. 5–7.

First line: "It started with a pooper-scooper."

The pitch: Shawn and Russell are best friends. They call themselves the PS Brothers. "PS is for Poop and Scoop." That's what the boys' business is all about. Shawn buys a pooper-scooper even though he doesn't have a dog. He wants one, though. He dreams of sharing a dog with his friend Russell. "A mean one. Not mean to us, but to anyone who tried to mess with us, take stuff from us, or say bad things about our families." They find a shady character named Nick who looks "like Jesus' evil twin." Nick is selling rottweiler puppies for $200 each. Shawn and Russell come up with a moneymaking plan to charge dog owners ten cents for every poop they pick up and dispose. "Big dogs cost double—twenty cents. Gigantic dogs cost a quarter."

Reading selection: Read the first two-thirds of chapter 8. A kid at their middle school finds the boys' business flyer and soon all the other kids tease them. "Shawn and I were . . . sick, freaks, ghetto, dweebs, losers, who . . . lived in a trash can, Dumpster, shack, with our convicts, bum relatives, and who . . . scooped poop for a living and wore clothes that even the thrift store wouldn't give away." The boys keep plugging away at their business. They find a lot of customers, enough so that they keep a list of bad dog owners they refuse to do further business with. "The owner who didn't tell us that her schnauzer had a bad case of diarrhea. The Chihuahua who had a thing for hiding under lawn furniture and then dashing out to attack ankles. The house where a lady asked us to walk her monstrous, leash-breaking mastiff, Bruno, after scooping, and she only gave us a quarter extra." When the boys go to Nick's place to make another payment toward their puppy, they find a lot of cars, men yelling, and dogs barking, growling, and yelping. End the selection where Shawn whispers, "It's something bad, Russ."

Read-alike recommendation: *The Meanest Hound Around* by Carol Wallace and Bill Wallace (Simon & Schuster, 2003) is the story of an abandoned dog that helps another dog escape from a mean junkyard owner.

Hecht, Tracey. *The Mysterious Abductions* (Nocturnals series). Fabled Films Press, 2016. Gr. 3–6.

First line: "As the first light of day surged above the horizon, Tobin crept toward home."

The pitch: Tobin is heading home to sleep after a long night. Tobin is a nocturnal animal, a creature that is awake and busy during the night. He is a pangolin, a weird little mammal with scales and a long tongue. He emits a gross stench every so often. Tobin meets Bismark, a sassy sugar glider, similar to a flying squirrel, and a fox named Dawn. All nocturnal animals. After the three defeat a menacing snake, they form a team they call the Nocturnal Brigade. They immediately find themselves on a mission after hearing a scream in the middle of the night. Something is snatching nocturnal animals: raccoons, possums, wombats, minks, honey badgers, kiwis, and even coyotes.

Reading selection: Read chapter 15, "The Abduction." Bismark, the sugar glider, has confronted the coyotes for the first time. He is convinced they are going to eat him. "Stand back! I can see hunger in your eyes! There is very little meat on these bones, I'll have you know." The other animals try to reassure Bismark that the coyotes are allies. They all press the sugar glider to tell them any information he might have learned about the missing nocturnal animals. Bismark faints under the questioning. The bats snicker and call him a featherweight until another scream in the distance causes everyone to run and try to locate the sound. When they return, they find an injured Tobin who says, "'They got him!' he sputtered. 'They took Bismark!'"

Read-alike recommendations: The sequel is *The Creeping Dark* (2016). *The Taken* by Inbali Iserles (Scholastic, 2015) is the story of a fox that develops powers to help survive in a cruel world. This is the first book in the Foxcraft series. The second title is *The Elders* (2016).

Hiaasen, Carl. *Chomp.* Knopf, 2012. Gr. 5–7.

First line: "Mickey Cray had been out of work ever since a dead iguana fell from a palm tree and hit him on the head."

The pitch: A kid named Wahoo—that's right, his name is Wahoo (his dad named him after a pro wrestler)—and his parents run a wildlife business in Florida. They rent alligators, pythons, snapping turtles, bobcats, and other critters to movie and television productions. Wahoo is known around school as someone not to mess with. He lost a thumb to an alligator named Alice. Wahoo and his father take a job working for Derek Bodger, the star of a popular, but totally fake, wilderness survival show. Wahoo's father keeps referring to Bodger as "His Phoniness." Trying to boost his ratings, Bodger decides to interact with real wild animals for once, not the tamer specimens. Bodger "was very much looking forward to being poked, stung, scratched, clawed, chewed and chomped by authentic denizens of the Everglades. And he would get his wish."

Reading selection: Read the second half of chapter 15, beginning with the sentence: "The Florida mastiff bat is the largest in the southeastern United States, reaching a length of almost seven inches." A female mastiff bat crashes into the camp of the production crew, perhaps confused by the sounds and bright lights. Bodger grabs the bat and holds it up, ready to eat it raw with the cameras rolling. The bat has other plans. "She reacted defensively and without hesitation. She chomped down on the first chompable target that came within reach, which happed to be Derek's plump, purple-blotched tongue. 'Aaaieeeeeegh! Aaaieeeeeeeeeeeeeeeeeeegh!'" The passage ends with Wahoo's father tickling the bat on its belly. Finish with the sentence: "With a shudder, the bat unhooked its fangs from Derek's swelling tongue."

Read-alike recommendations: Hiaasen has several other animal- and ecology-themed action stories including *Hoot* (2002), *Flush* (2005), *Scat* (2009), and *Skink—No Surrender* (2014).

Jennings, Patrick. *We Can't All Be Rattlesnakes.* HarperCollins, 2009. Gr. 4–6.

First line: "I had shed a skin the day of my capture."

The pitch: A gopher snake tries her best to escape a young boy who picks her up with a stick and grabs her behind the jaws. "'You got a good grip there,' the kid said. 'Think I'll call you Crusher.'" The boy, Gunnar, is a very unlikable kid. In addition to Crusher, Gunnar keeps a tarantula, a desert tortoise, and an alligator lizard in separate boxes in his room. The tortoise tells Crusher that "when the boy brings home a new animal, he's very excited by it. He sits and watches it through the glass for long periods of time. But pretty soon he gets bored and starts tormenting it." Crusher vows to never be the boy's pet. She goes on a hunger strike, even ignoring the live mouse he puts in her cage. She starts calling the mouse Breakfast even though she refuses to eat it. 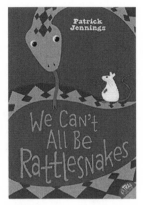 Gunnar's friends Byron and Matthew come over to see his new snake. Byron insists Crusher is a male and begs to hold the snake. "I won't sue if he bites, I swear on the Bible." Crusher proceeds to bite Byron, who screams and hollers, "What's the number for 911?" Gunnar takes Crusher to school for a pet parade. Different judges come over to look at his "pet."

Reading selection: Read the last half of chapter 8, "Scariest," with the line: "We are about to begin the judging." A teacher named Ms. Japecki is startled when Crusher lunges at her. "'Is th-that l-l-lid on t-tight?' she asked Gunnar." Gunnar is delighted Crusher freaked her out and does a victory dance when Crusher wins the Scariest Pet award. The chapter ends with Crusher thinking, "My plan was working. He was seeing me as a loyal pet. With luck, soon I could ditch him."

Read-alike recommendation: The book *Hiss-s-s-s!* by Eric Kimmel (Holiday House, 2012) features a boy named Omar who convinces his parents to buy him a corn snake as a pet.

Keating, Jess. *Pink Is for Blobfish: Discovering the World's Perfectly Pink Animals.* **Knopf, 2016. Gr. 3–4.**

First line: "Think you know pink?"

The pitch: Pink is not just a color for princesses. It could also mean danger. The dragon millipede is pink and its color means "back off." The dragon millipede secretes a toxic chemical called hydrogen cyanide if a predator tries to bite it. Sometimes the color pink is used as camouflage to hide itself. The orchid mantis blends in with flowers so it can catch insects to eat. Its pink appearance also hides it from predators, like birds and bats, that want to eat it. Watch out for the pinktoe tarantula. Ironically, it's bright blue when it hatches. Other little pink creatures include the southern blind snake and

pink slugs. There are pink mammals including the Amazon River dolphin, the naked mole rat, the red uakari monkey (it has a pink head to attract potential mates), and something called the pink fairy armadillo. The book also describes many pink sea creatures like the pygmy seahorse, the Hopkins' rose nudibranch (basically a sea snail without the shell), pink sea stars, hairy squat lobsters (how's that for a name), and the title animal—the blobfish.

Reading selection: Read the one-page entry for the blobfish. Each creature profile begins with a paragraph of facts, followed by an amusing attribute of the animal. The blobfish is made of "gelatinous goo" and drifts in the ocean "like bloated pink balloons." When it eats, it simply opens its mouth, and food—snails, worms, crustaceans—float in. It doesn't have any predators but it is in danger of extinction because blobfish often get caught in fishing nets. Another name for the blobfish is "fathead sculpin. These fish can't catch a break." The blobfish was "voted the ugliest animal in the world in a poll taken by the Ugly Animal Preservation Society."

Read-alike recommendation: Living Color by Steve Jenkins (Houghton Mifflin, 2007) is a nicely laid-out, clear-to-follow picture book that groups animals together by color.

MacLachlan, Patricia. *White Fur Flying*. Margaret K. McElderry, 2013. Gr. 3–5.

First line: "'Once upon a time there was a wicked queen,' said my younger sister, Alice."

The pitch: Alice is sharing a fairy tale with her family and two Great Pyrenees dogs named Kodi and May. The family cares for dogs until new homes can be found for them. While Alice is spinning her story, they all spot a sad little boy go into the neighbors' house. The boy, Phillip, doesn't speak. He is staying with the Cassidys, the new neighbors, while "his parents solve a problem." Alice thinks Mrs. Cassidy is mean. Alice's mom thinks Mrs. Cassidy is afraid of dogs, and also . . . Phillip. Zoe and Alice's family have a parrot named Lena. Zoe remarks, "There's a boy next door who doesn't talk and a parrot inside who talks all the time."

Reading selection: Read chapter 8. Alice and Zoe take Lena's cage outside to sit with Phillip and Kodi. Lena sees cows for the first time and squawks. Alice says, "She doesn't know what cows are. She has no words for them." Zoe tells Phillip that Lena wants him to talk to her. She and Alice walk away to give Phillip and Lena some privacy. "'Phillip will talk when he has something important to say, I suppose,' said Alice." The girls' mother returns home with two new dogs, Callie and Jack. The dogs run down and join Phillip in the yard. End the selection just short of the end of the chapter with the sentence: "Phillip and Jack sat quietly, watching the cows move in the green grass of the meadow, under a blue cloudless sky."

Read-alike recommendations: The Animal Rescue Team series by Sue Stauffacher follows a family that takes in a variety of rescued animals. The titles in this series are *Gator on the Loose!* (Knopf, 2010), *Special Delivery!* (2010), *Hide and Seek* (2010), and *Show Time* (2011).

McKay, Hilary. *Lulu and the Duck in the Park*. Albert Whitman, 2011. Gr. 3–4.

First lines: "Lulu was famous for animals. Her famousness for animals was known throughout the whole neighborhood."

The pitch: Lulu's fascination with animals includes all members of the animal kingdom from "the sponsored polar bear family that had been her best Christmas present, to the hairiest unwanted spider in the school coat room." That's fine with her parents as long as Lulu follows her "mother's law on pets. The More, the Merrier As Long as Lulu Cleans up after Them." Lulu not only cleans up after animals, she talks to them, exercises them, feeds them, researches them, and constantly thinks about them. She goes so far as to provide the spiders in her house with "a little rope ladder to help them out of the bath." Every Tuesday, Lulu's class goes to the town park to play and swim. Lulu loves to share her treat with one particular white-winged brown duck.

Reading selection: Start reading halfway through chapter 2, "Morning in the Park," with the lines: "That was what usually happened on Tuesdays. But this Tuesday was different." All the ducks in the park have nests. Two enormous dogs run loose, chasing ducks and smashing nests. Lulu spots one duck egg rolling down a grassy slope. The chapter ends with the lines: "Before Mellie turned around, before anyone saw, before she even thought what she was doing, Lulu had picked it up and put it in her pocket. It was still warm."

Read-alike recommendations: Lulu's fascination with animals continues in the following sequels: *Lulu and the Dog from the Sea* (2013), *Lulu and the Cat in the Bag* (2013), *Lulu and the Rabbit Next Door* (2014), *Lulu and the Hedgehog in the Rain* (2014), and *Lulu and the Hamster in the Night* (2015).

Nippert-Eng, Christena. *Gorillas Up Close*. Holt, 2016. Gr. 4–7.

First lines: "Gorillas. What's not to love?"

The pitch: North American zoos are home to approximately 350 gorillas today. Kwan, a silverback, an adult male, is profiled with several other gorillas, many who live in the Lincoln Park Zoo in Chicago. He weighs 365 pounds and eats sixteen pounds of vegetables, leafy greens, and fruit each day. For a snack, he might get low-sugar breakfast cereal. Despite his enormous size, Kwan "can pick up a single Rice Krispie with those great sausage fingers of his." We learn interesting facts like "a gorilla's nose is like a human fingerprint. No two are exactly alike." If you watch gorillas in the zoo, don't show your teeth. "Showing teeth can be a sign of aggression among adult gorillas." Gorillas will laugh but they don't show their teeth while doing so. Staring at gorillas isn't cool, either.

Move your eyes and your body every once in a while, otherwise the gorillas will think you're up to no good.

Reading selection: Read the chapter titled "Teenagers." Gorilla teenagers are called "blackbacks." As they grow older they'll become "silverbacks." Blackbacks help silverbacks protect the family, mostly by patrolling the edges of the group. They help silverbacks solve problems, like when poachers threaten them in the wild. A park ranger tells of the time he went to dismantle poacher traps. A silverback grunted a warning, so the ranger stopped and watched. Two juveniles, a male and a female, dismantled one trap and, with the help of a blackback, dismantled another one. The chapter ends with the line: "They seemed to have learned how to handle the traps by watching their dad."

Read-alike recommendation: Gorilla Doctors: Saving Endangered Great Apes by Pamela S. Turner (Houghton Mifflin, 2005) is another nonfiction book full of color photographs featuring different aspects of gorillas.

Rocha, K. E. *Secrets of Bearhaven*. Scholastic, 2016. Grades 4–6.

First lines: "*Roooaaaaaarrr!* Spencer Plain raced through the forest, his heart pounding. He dodged trees and skidded across patches of slick moss, trying desperately not to fall. Now was *not* the time to fall. There was a bear behind him."

The pitch: Spencer is clearly confused when his uncle Mark pulls up at school in his red Porsche and yells for him to grab his stuff and hop in. Spencer learns that his parents, who are both world travelers working for a group called Paws for Peace, a group that helps keep bears safe, have gone missing. Spencer is further confused when Uncle Mark tells him they have to reach a safe place. None of this makes sense to Spencer. He really freaks out when he learns they are being followed. A black Corvette, no license plates, is chasing them. At the last minute, Uncle Mark pulls to the side of the road and commands Spencer to run as fast as he can into the forest.

Reading selection: Go back to the first chapter and pick up where you left off with the opening lines. Begin with the sentence: "Spencer had taken one look at the bear, heard that ferocious roar, and set off running as fast as he could, but the huge animal was gaining on him." While running, Spencer tries to remember if bears eat humans. He falls down a steep hill and bumps to a stop. He lies on his back, listening for any sign of the bear. He is sure he has gotten away. Just as he sits up, a big black paw holds him in place. End the passage with the following lines: "'Spencer Plain,' the bear growled. 'We have been expecting you.'"

Read-alike recommendations: The sequels are *Mission to Moonfarm* (2016) and *Hidden Rock Rescue* (2016). *The Secret Zoo* by Bryan Chick (Greenwillow, 2010) is another fantasy where humans interact with animals. At a zoo, a girl named Megan disappears through a secret entrance to a land where humans live side by side with animals. Its sequels are *Search and Shadows* (2011), *Riddles and Dangers* (2011), *Traps and Specters* (2012), and *Raids and Rescues* (2013).

CHAPTER 10

Sports

While sports books as a genre aren't as universally popular with a wide audience, those kids who love to read about sports figures really, really get into these books. A variety of sports are covered as well as sports books including both gender protagonists and biographies as well.

Abdul-Jabbar, Kareem, and Raymond Obstfeld. *Sasquatch in the Paint* **(Streetball Crew series). Hyperion, 2013. Gr. 5–7.**

First lines: "Hey, Chewbacca! How do you say 'loser' in Wookie?"

The pitch: Thirteen-year-old Theo is six foot four inches. Yup, six-four at the age of thirteen. Theo grew six inches over the summer. Of course, he has attracted the attention of the school basketball coach. He's not a good basketball player but he's flattered to be recruited. Theo is still getting used to his growth spurt. "His legs had grown so suddenly that he felt a little wobbly on them, like he was walking on shaky stilts." The author knows all about this because he is legendary NBA star Kareem Abdul-Jabbar. The opposing players quickly learn that Theo is all height and no skills. The opposing team's fans target him with their insults. "Hey freak, loved you in *Avatar*!" "Stop calling him Bigfoot! He prefers to be called by his proper name: Sasquatch!" That last taunt was shouted by Theo's classmate, a new girl, a girl named Rain, a girl who mistakenly wound up on the opposing fans' bleachers.

Reading selection: Read chapter 4. It opens with Rain saying, "Man, you sure stank up the court today." She mocks him for not knowing NBA basketball legend Dr. J. He retorts that she doesn't know Magnus Carlsen, Levon Aronian, and Vladimir Kramnik. She shocks him when she correctly says they are the "three top-ranked chess players in the world." A black-leathered biker roars up and hollers at Rain in a foreign language. He slaps her when she tells him to mind his own business. Rain kicks the guy in the shins. When Theo runs toward him, the biker takes off. Rain takes off as well. The chapter ends with her yelling, "See you around, Sasquatch."

Read-alike recommendations: Author Abdul-Jabbar's *Stealing the Game* (2015) is a companion book that focuses on Chris, a kid from Theo's team. Chris's older brother Jax gets into trouble betting on basketball games. *Hustle* by Johnny Boateng (Lorimer, 2014) is another fast-paced sports story about a young basketball player nicknamed "Hustle."

Coy, John. *Top of the Order* (4 for 4 series). Feiwel & Friends, 2009. Gr. 4–6.

First lines: "Outside my classroom window, green grass glistens on the first day of May. May means baseball season and baseball season means me."

The pitch: Fifth grader Jackson plays shortstop. His friends Gig—short for "whirligig" because he is in constant motion—and Jessie are looking for players to fill out their summer baseball team. They all worry about middle school. They heard that the school pool is full of germs, students have to take naked showers after swimming, the teachers are mean, and bullies beat up kids. "'Did you hear that some eighth graders make you drink a Coke so fast, you hurl in the garbage can?' Gig jams a potato triangle into his mouth." Gig adds that the bullies then "push your face right into the puke." He finishes entertaining everyone by sticking mini corn dogs up his nose. The boys recruit new kid Diego, who moved from Texas, and are now looking for someone to play second base. To Gig's dismay, the best candidate turns out to be his sister Sydney.

Reading selection: Read chapter 6. Sydney shows up to baseball practice. She already checked with the league. There's a rule that states, "If a sport is not available for girls, girls can play on the boys' team." The coach lets Sydney try out. She misses her first few ground balls and complains about her new glove. "'I'm not used to it. Let me get my regular glove.' She runs to her pack and pulls out another one—a bright pink glove." She doesn't miss a single ball after that and makes the team as their new second baseman. Gig is still upset. "Believe me, Barf Breath's a disaster. She thinks she's smarter than anyone else. She'll start telling all of us what to do. She'll try to run the team." The chapter ends with Gig saying, "'Jackson'—he turns as he rides away—'do what you can to force her out.'"

Read-alike recommendations: The four friends appear again in *Eyes on the Goal* (2010) where they play soccer, *Love of the Game* (2011), a book about football, and finally *Take Your Best Shot* (2012), when the boys play on the basketball team. Author Coy has also written two sports fiction books for slightly older readers. *Crackback* (Scholastic, 2005) follows a high school football team and *Box Out* (2008), a high school basketball team.

Green, Michelle Y. *A Strong Right Arm: The Story of Mamie "Peanut" Johnson.* **Dial, 2002. Gr. 4–7.**

First line: "Mama never mentioned it, but I'm sure I musta been born with a baseball in my hand, its smooth white skin curving into my tiny brown palm."

The pitch: In this biography, we learn that Mamie Johnson was one of only three women to ever play professional baseball. She got her nickname when an opposing batter looked at her five-foot-two-inch frame and mockingly said she was no bigger than a peanut. After she struck him out, Mamie yelled, "Call me Peanut." Mamie grew up playing baseball in South Carolina where first base was a pie plate, second base was a piece of a flowerpot, a lilac bush was third, and home plate was the lid of a sugar bucket. When she moved to New Jersey, kids taunted her. "You're just a dumb old girl, and you're colored besides." She shut them up when they saw her pitch. She had a "surefire windup, coming-right-at-ya pitch smack dab over the plate."

Reading selection: Read most of the chapter titled "Bannecker Field," beginning with the lines: "'Look,' Rita said to me as I was fixing to take the mound at the top of the ninth inning. 'There he is again!'" She points out a baseball scout. The opposing team's best hitter faces Mamie. He "extended his arm straight out and pointed his bat right at me like some playground bully. I don't know if he was trying to make me mad or just scare the stripes right off my uniform, but I knew it was exactly the wrong thing to do." After Mamie strikes him out, the scout invites her to try out for the Indianapolis Clowns, a professional Negro League baseball team. He tells her, "They're looking for new talent—someone to make the crowd stand up and take notice. I think you might be just the ticket."

Read-alike recommendation: 42: The Jackie Robinson Story by Aaron Rosenberg (Scholastic, 2013) is the movie novelization of another legendary African American baseball player who broke the color barrier.

Green, Tim. *New Kid.* **Harper, 2014. Gr. 5–7.**

First line: "Tommy knew from the beginning that this moment was going to be special, the kind that could change his life forever."

The pitch: Tommy Rust already hit one home run in the championship game. He has a 3–2 count on him in the bottom of the final inning when his father suddenly appears and yanks him out of the game. Tommy's father is on the run. There are men after him. Tommy knows little about his father's life except that his mother was killed because of his father's activities. Tommy knows, too, that he can no longer be Tommy Rust. Once they arrive at their new home in upstate New York, Tommy's new name is Brock Nickerson. Brock has a run-in with the school bully Nagel, a kid half the size of Brock but a tough fighter nonetheless. Coach Hudgens breaks up their fight. Nagel warms up to Brock and convinces him to help vandalize Coach's house. Coach catches Brock in the act and not only forgives him, but teaches Brock how to pitch. Despite the fact that Brock is starting to fit in with his new surroundings, trouble is not far behind.

Reading selection: Read the last part of chapter 30, beginning with the line: "They began picking up the balls, plunking them into the bucket in silence, when something abruptly banged the fence." Someone is throwing rocks at Coach and Brock. Continue reading the two-page chapter 31. While Coach is still out looking for the culprits, Brock finds himself surrounded by older teens, led by Nagel's brother Jamie. Read into chapter 32. Jamie hits Brock in the head. Brock is saved from further damage when "from nowhere, a white streak whistled through the small crowd. THUNK. Jamie Nagel's chest rang out like a bass drum. He dropped to the grass along with the baseball that hit him in the middle of his back." Jamie and his gang run off. Nagel tells Brock and Coach that he tried to stop his brother and then he, too, runs off. End the reading where Coach warns Brock, "You know, when you lie down with dogs, you get up with fleas."

Read-alike recommendation: The sequel *First Team* (2014) finds Brock still on the run with his father. At their new home, Brock tries out for quarterback for his new school's football team.

Kelly, David A. *The Gold Medal Mess* (MVP series). Random House, 2016. Gr. 3–4.

First line: "Max stared at the big round target on the other side of the gym."

The pitch: Max and Alice are shooting arrows to practice for their school's annual Olympics. Max finds an envelope that reads: "BEWARE! CANCEL YOUR OLYMPICS!" Inside is another message: "YOUR OLYMPICS ARE A JOKE. CANCEL THEM, OR THE JOKE WILL BE ON YOU!" Mr. Hardy, the principal, thinks that someone is simply playing a joke, but Max decides to conduct an investigation with the help of his friends. Meanwhile, the school Olympics go on.

Reading selection: Read chapter 5, "The Torch Relay Tangle." The first Olympic event has a fun twist to it. Mr. Hardy tells the crowd that for the torch relay, "instead of using real flaming torches, we decided to have the students use toilet plungers!" The kids line up and each team is handed a plunger. The goal of the race is for the kids "to run to the orange cones on the other side of the field and back before handing the plunger to the next person in line. The first group to have all their runners cross the line would be the winner." The race begins and Max and Alice's teammate Kat gets an early lead. As the leaders round the orange cones, they flip into the air and onto the ground. When they try to stand up, they slide again and "flipped onto their backs. Their toilet plungers went flying!" Mr. Hardy and other teachers run to help, and they also tumble down. The school janitor discovers the grass is covered in cooking oil. The kids think it was done to sabotage the Olympics and they look for clues. The chapter ends with the lines: "The adults were almost finished moving the cones when Kat spoke up. 'Bingo!' she called out to the others. 'I found something. Come here, quick!'"

Read-alike recommendations: The MVP kids return in *The Soccer Surprise* (2016) and *The Football Fumble* (2016). *Sabotage Season* by Alex Morgan (Simon & Schuster, 2013) is another sports story where a girls' soccer team deals with sabotage.

LeGrand, Eric. *Believe: The Victorious Story of Eric LeGrand*. Harper, 2012. Gr. 5–7.

First line: "I am constantly cold."

The pitch: Eric LeGrand's body feels cold ever since his injury. In this autobiography, we learn that Eric has been paralyzed. "Take a simple thing like an itching nose. Before the injury, I'd rub my nose with one of my fingers and that would take care of the itch. Now I had to scrunch up my nose, wiggle my mouth, and stretch my facial muscles to satisfy the itch, but usually those actions didn't cut it." Today, Eric gives school presentations about his life. He says, "The middle schoolers hung on every word, and I think it's because most kids have never been around someone in a wheelchair." He tells them about the injury. Eric was on football special team kickoff coverage, or as he says, "My job was to sprint down the field while the ball was in the air and annihilate any blocker, fill any running lanes, and knock the kick returner to the ground." Eric remembers, "The time was 4:46 Eastern Standard Time on October 6, 2010—a moment that will forever be etched in my mind."

Reading selection: Begin reading chapter 9, "The Collision." Eric is in full sprint against the Army college team's kickoff returner, Malcolm Brown. He slips past two defenders. Eric's helmet hits Brown's collarbone, and there is "a sickening sound that ricocheted through the stadium." Eric's "body instantly went stiff." He knows something is bad right away. He thinks he might have received a stinger or a concussion. He tries to get up, but his body won't move at all. Eric has trouble breathing. He can't talk to the trainers kneeling by his side. End the passage with the line: "It's bad, man."

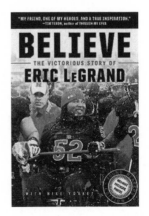

Read-alike recommendation: Paralyzed by Jeff Rud (Orca, 2008) is the fictional account of football

paralysis. Reggie is accused of being a dirty player because of seriously damaging an opposing football player in a game.

Lemke, Donnie. *Drop In* (Tony Hawk's 900 Revolution series). Stone Arch, 2012. Gr. 5–7.

First line: "On July 27, 1999 . . . Tony Hawk landed the first-ever 900."

The pitch: Legend has it that shortly after this historic moment, a force shattered Hawk's skateboard and "everything changed." Omar and Tommy are two friends who grew up like brothers. "They shared a love of skateboarding, primo fish tacos, beach bunnies, and punk rock." Tommy insults a street vendor who retaliates with a "SPL-AT! A large, black garbage bag struck Tommy in the back of the head, splitting open and covering him in a gooey mess." After Tommy spits out the fish juice, he and Omar continue recording each other. Tommy goads Omar. "What kind of sponsor would shell out for some no-namer poppin' nollies and heelflips down a 5-stair? You gotta go big, Omar, or you ain't going anywhere but home."

Reading selection: Read chapter 2. It opens with the lines: "Without hesitation, Omar took off on his skateboard. Tommy followed closely behind, trying hard to keep up and keep Omar in the viewfinder's frame." The two arrive at the Imperial Beach Pier where Omar announces he'll do the Imperial 5-0. He will skate the length of the Imperial Pier, do a 5-0 grind on the safety rail, and return without falling the five-story height into the Pacific. Omar skates past the "No Skateboarding" signs and spots a six-foot section of the wooden safety rail. Omar ollies high into the air, lands on the rail, and as he prepares to end his trick, a large bird swoops by and kills Omar's concentration. Omar heads for the water. The chapter ends with the lines: "As the dark ocean water quickly approached, Omar realized that rising from this fall would require some kind of miracle. Then everything went black."

Read-alike recommendations: The other books in the series are *Impulse* by M. Zachary Sherman (2012), *Fall Line* by M. Zachary Sherman (2012), *Unchained* by M. Zachary Sherman (2012), *Amplified* by Blake A. Hoena (2012), *Tunnel Vision* by Brandon Terrell (2012), *Exiled* by Brandon Terrell (2012), *Lockdown* by Matthew K. Manning (2012), *Zombified* by Blake A. Hoena (2012), *Unearthed* by Brandon Terrell (2013), *Flipside* by Brandon Terrell (2013), *Recharged* by Brandon Terrell (2013), and *Horizon* by Brandon Terrell (2013).

Mancusi, Mari. *Golden Girl*. Aladdin, 2015. Gr. 5–7.

First lines: "One year ago . . . Ladies and gentlemen! Next up in the seventeenth annual Parent's Day Competition here at Mountain Academy, we have four very talented athletes competing in the snowboard cross event."

The pitch: Seventh grader Lexi is one of the four competitors. Her archenemy Olivia snarls, "You just watch yourself, *Golden Girl*." During the race, Lexi feels someone tugging her back and she loses her balance. As she hits a tree, Lexi thinks, "I'm sorry, Dad," and blacks out. One year later, Lexi returns to Mountain Academy, a school that has produced thirty-six Winter Olympic medalists over the years. She says, "Hanging out with my friends on the beach, tanning and talking and flirting with cute lifeguards sounded so much better than freezing my butt off up here while trying to chase my dream for a second time."

Reading selection: Start reading halfway into chapter 5, with the line: "I knew in my head there was no shame in it; in fact, any normal person would think it was a smart and sensible thing to do—to take it easy and find my feet before jumping off the deep end." Unfortunately for her, Lexi's "fellow students weren't normal people—they were total sharks, and any hint of blood in the snow would spark a feeding frenzy." Lexi is goaded into trying the challenging snowboard park. She takes off but finds that her body is not in shape yet. She wipes out. The chapter ends with the following passage: "But no, nothing seemed to be injured. Except, of course, my pride. Not to mention my hopes and dreams. And my golden snowboarding career, which now had officially turned to tin."

Read-alike recommendation: Snowboard Hero by Jake Maddox (Stone Arch, 2015) is about thirteen-year-old Kaleb who wants to honor his wounded soldier brother by competing on a difficult slopestyle course.

Scaletta, Kurtis. *Jinxed!* (A Topps League Story series). Amulet, 2012. Gr. 3–4.

First line: "I was just a kid, but I already had my dream job."

The pitch: Chad's dream job is to be the batboy for the Pine City Porcupines. It's a job he really, really wants. His father tells him to send the team a resume. Chad asks, "What's a rez-u-may?" His father explains that it's a list of Chad's jobs and accomplishments. Chad lists facts like "I have more than 5,000 baseball cards" and "I learned every Porcupine player's name last year" and "I have my own resume." He gets an interview with the clubhouse manager, Wally, and shows up wearing a snap-on tie. Chad impresses Wally, who hires him on the spot but warns, "No more ties. Don't you know there are no ties in baseball?" Chad is surprised to learn that his classmate Dylan has also been chosen as a batboy.

Reading selection: Read chapter 3. Chad and Dylan show up at Pine City Park to meet the team bus. The bus pulls up and the players get off one by one. The players try to freak out the boys by warning them about a giant rat on the bus. One player even makes a loud rat noise. "EEEK, EEEK, EEEK!" The last player off the bus is the rookie Tommy. "He yawned, blinked, then looked at us. His nose was all black. There were whiskers on his face. His baseball cap had big round ears attached to it." Chad tells him, "You've got rat stuff on your face."

Tommy groans. "Oh, man. That's what I get for falling asleep on the bus." At the end of the chapter, Chad is ready to ride his bike home when he sees that "something was pawing at the ground in the shadows by the right field wall." He hopes it's not a dog, coyote, or bear. The chapter ends with the lines: "The shadow stopped and turned toward me. It looked up at me in surprise. I looked back in just as much surprise. *Huh?*"

Read-alike recommendations: The other books in the series are *Steal That Base!* (2012), *Zip It!* (2012), *The 823rd Hit* (2012), *You're Out!* (2013), and *Batter Up!* (2013).

Stabler, David. *Kid Athletes: True Tales of Childhood from Sports Legends* (Kid Legends series). Quirk, 2015. Gr. 3–6.

First lines: "Not all great athletes are born great. In fact, some of them start out downright bad."

The pitch: George Herman, later known as Babe Ruth, grew up in "the roughest, toughest saloon in the city of Baltimore." His father owned the bar and his parents often left George to roam the streets alone. He sometimes "threw eggs and rotten apples at the carriage drivers as they passed." His parents sent him to St. Mary's Industrial School for Orphans, Delinquent, Incorrigible, and Wayward Boys. George was labeled as incorrigible. That means there's little hope the person will ever behave properly. At his new home, George was given some tough love by Brother Matthias, who introduced the lad to baseball. Years later, Babe Ruth's wife said, "When Babe Ruth was twenty-three, the world loved him. When he was thirteen, only Brother Matthias loved him." Not all of the sports figures profiled in this book had rough beginnings, but all faced some sort of challenge. Football quarterback Peyton Manning, race car driver Danica Patrick, basketball player Yao Ming, boxing legend Muhammad Ali, and gymnast Gabby Douglas are just a few athletes profiled. Here's another sports legend. . . .

Reading selection: Read the chapter titled "Bruce Lee: The Kung Fu Kid." Bruce was born in San Francisco and grew up in Hong Kong. One time he dressed up as a girl because of a Chinese superstition that demons kidnap boys. Two kids made fun of him during a ferry ride. "At first, Bruce kept his cool, but as soon as the boat docked, he charged the two boys, kicking one in the shin and sending the other fleeing in terror." Kids learned not to mess with Bruce. He often skipped school and joined a gang. Finally, thirteen-year-old Bruce took lessons from kung fu master Yip Man and "took all the energy he used to spend playing pranks and fighting and applied it to studying the finer points of kung fu." He eventually made it back to America where he became a big movie star.

Read-alike recommendation: The Kids Legends series includes *Kid Presidents: True Tales of Childhood from America's Presidents* (2014) and *Kid Artists: True Tales of Childhood from Creative Legends* (2016).

CHAPTER 11

Other Fascinating People

This section is composed of biographies not already covered under the Animals and Sports sections of this book. Some of the books are collective biographies, several short biographies of the lives of several people in one book, and others focus solely on one individual. I still remember one man, now in his twenties, who told me that he never read anything as a child until he discovered biographies.

Bragg, Georgia. *How They Croaked: The Awful Ends of the Awfully Famous.* Walker, 2011. Gr. 5–7.

First line: "Warning: If you don't have the guts for gore, do not read this book."

The pitch: This book is "full of bad news. There are funny crying parts and disgusting stupid parts and hideous cool parts, but it's pretty much one train wreck after another." Weird things happened to a few of these historical celebrities' bodies after they died. King Tut's brains were broken apart by a hooked bronze needle that was stuck up his nose and pulled out one piece at a time (Tut died of malaria). Fans of Galileo Galilei stole three of his fingers, a vertebra, and a toe (Galileo died of lead poisoning). Albert Einstein's whole brain was stolen by a pathologist who stored it in his basement in a beer cooler for several years (Einstein died of a burst artery). And Marie Antoinette, who was beheaded by a guillotine, had her head tossed on the grass while the grave diggers took a lunch break. This allowed the famous wax modeler Marie Tussaud "time to sculpt her face in wax before she was put in the ground." What folks did to George Washington while he was still alive is even worse.

Reading selection: Read the chapter titled "George Washington: Little Mouth of Horrors." When the father of the country woke up one morning, he was having trouble breathing. While waiting for the doctor, his overseer and secretary cut into a vein to let out a half a pint of blood. "Doctors thought bad blood accumulated and stagnated in the body and needed to be removed." When the doctor finally arrived, he smeared the ground-up remains of a highly poisonous beetle across Washington's neck before draining the neck. Another doctor came. They spread more beetle potion and did more bloodletting. "A total of about 80 ounces of blood came out of George Washington." They gave him solutions to throw up and to go to the bathroom. It was later determined an infection on the back of his tongue that protects the windpipe is what really killed Washington. "Today, a simple dose of antibiotics would have cured him."

Read-alike recommendation: Author Bragg uses a similar format for the book *How They Choked: Failures, Flops, and Flaws of the Awfully Famous* (2014).

Hodgman, Ann. *How to Die of Embarrassment Every Day*. Holt, 2011. Gr. 4–6.

First lines: "This isn't a regular book. You don't have to read the chapters in order. As a matter of fact, they're not exactly chapters. Some of them are so short that they're more like paragraphs, or what magazine editors call 'boxes.' Some are so short that you need a microscope to see them."

The pitch: Children's author Ann Hodgman was born in 1956 and acknowledges, "Yes, I realize that 1956 sounds like a fake year to you." She uses the real names for the people she didn't say anything bad about, fake names for those people who might be embarrassed by what she shares, and also fake names for those people who might get mad "and come after me." Ann's first memory is of the time she was two and a half years old and reached up to the top of a stove and burned her wrist on the pilot light. Another memory is when a bullet flew past her face while she was reading in bed. Ann also shares the story of when she pushed over a neighbor kid's snowman simply because she felt, "We've seen that snowman for long enough." Once, she asked her father if she could hit a squirrel with a rock and then nurse it back to health. Funny, weird little memories. And, as the title promises, there were some memories that were embarrassing.

Reading selection: Read the section titled "Nicknames." As an adult, Ann heard a children's song called "I Hate My Name." She found that the song "got lodged in my brain" and was singing it out loud when she realized their house-painter was listening to her, a grown woman, singing "I Hate My Name." Ann says, "There was no way he could have missed my singing—I was mooing like a cow." That got her to thinking of the time some kids gave her the nickname of Hampton Schnoz and told her she had a big nose. Ann worked hard to get kids to call her something else. The chapter ends with an adult memory. "By the way, when I grew up, I asked a plastic surgeon if she thought my nose was too big, and she said yes. But I'm going to leave it the way it is."

Read-alike recommendation: When I Was Your Age: Volumes I and II; Original Stories about Growing Up, edited by Amy Ehrlich (Candlewick, 2012) is about several children's authors who share childhood incidents, including Mary Pope Osborne, the author of the Magic Tree House books.

Philip, Aaron, and Tonya Bolden. *This Kid Can Fly: It's about Ability (NOT Disability)*. Balzer + Bray, 2016. Gr. 5–7.

First line: "So you're probably wondering: Who is this kid writing his memoir?"

The pitch: Meet Aaron, pronounced AY-run. He had a rough beginning. He was born in 2001 in the two-island nation of Antigua and Barbuda in the Caribbean. He was two and a half pounds at birth. His first bed was an incubator to help his underdeveloped lungs. Aaron was two months old before he was able to go home from the hospital. He was so tiny, his parents had to cut a pair of Pampers in half. In 2003, Aaron was diagnosed with "the incurable CP, cerebral palsy." He is not able to walk or run. At times, he was in "mind-blowing pain." Aaron and his mother moved to New York City where he received medical care. When he got too heavy for his mother, his father moved in as his primary caretaker. His mother moved back to the island to work and raise Aaron's brother. At one point, Aaron and his father had to live in a shelter. As he got older, Aaron "increasingly felt Completely and Totally Invisible (CATI)." He felt kids at his school "simply didn't get me." He started a blog he called *Aaronverse* that led to a presentation for the staff of Tumblr that was covered on *The Today Show*. He says, "I felt validated. Nobody was looking past me. Nobody was looking through me. Nobody was trying to avoid eye contact with me or making me feel like I made them uncomfortable, like I was some alien being." Aaron still had his challenges.

Reading selection: Read the very end of chapter 16, "*Tanda*," where Aaron describes his book and video creation. "*Tanda* is about a guy named, well, Tanda." Move on to chapter 17, "My Boys! My Boys!" Aaron's father suffers a heart attack. He makes it to the hospital, but Aaron and his brother are left alone overnight. Even though Aaron's father needs a triple bypass, he tries to leave against doctor's orders, worried about "My boys! My boys!" End the passage with the line: "As I told folks in *Aaronverse*, tsunamis of support rained down on the Philip boys."

Read-alike recommendation: Out of My Mind by Sharon Draper (Atheneum, 2010) is the fictional account of a young person with cerebral palsy. The main character, Melody, says, "I can't talk. I can't walk. I can't feed myself or take myself to the bathroom. Big bummer."

Pollack, Pam, and Meg Belviso. *Who Is J. K. Rowling?* **(Who Was . . . ? series) Grosset & Dunlap, 2012. Gr. 3–5.**

First line: "Do you know what a Muggle is?"

The pitch: Many people have no doubt heard of the muggle known as J. K. Rowling, but what do we know about her? Her first name is Jo. She added the "K" later after her grandmother Kathleen. Jo always wanted to be a writer. One day, while she was on a train, staring out the window, "suddenly a picture of a boy popped into her head. He had round glasses and a scar shaped like a lightning bolt." She didn't have a pen with her, but other characters flooded her head, characters like Nearly Headless Nick and Hermione. When she got home, she grabbed a pen and began writing about Harry Potter. When her mother developed multiple sclerosis, her friend Seán cheered her up. He became the inspiration for Ron Weasley. Jo added Seán's car into the series. "The car rescues Harry just as it had rescued Jo—only in Jo's imagination, the car could fly." Jo had a lanky, long-haired teacher who called her a "daydreamer." He was the inspiration behind Severus Snape. Jo found inspiration all around her.

Reading selection: Read the very end of chapter 2, "A Flying Car," with the sentence: "After leaving Wyedean in 1983, Jo attended the University of Exeter." She used her love of languages in her writing, even to develop character names "like Voldemort and Malfoy. In French, *mort* means death, *mal* means bad, and *foy* comes from *foi* which means faith." Read the accompanying "Character Names" chart that explains interesting facts about the Weasleys, Remus Lupin, Fenrir Greyback, Sirius Black, Albus Dumbledore, Rita Skeeter, and Peeves. For example, for Sirius Black, "Sirius is named after the dog star. Very fitting for a man who can turn into a dog!" And for Rita Skeeter, the annoying reporter, "*Skeeter* is a slang word for mosquito." As for the Weasleys? One of Jo's favorite animals is the weasel.

Read-alike recommendations: There are more biographies of children's authors in the extensive Who Was . . . ? series. These include *Who Was Dr. Seuss?* by Janet B. Pascal (2011), *Who Was Roald Dahl?* by True Kelley (2012), *Who Was Maurice Sendak?* by Janet B. Pascal (2013), *Who Was Beatrix Potter?* by Sarah Fabiny (2015), and *Who Is Jeff Kinney?* by Patrick Kinney (2015).

Romero, Jordan, and Linda LeBlanc. *No Summit Out of Sight: The True Story of the Youngest Person to Climb the Seven Summits.* **Simon & Schuster, 2014. Gr. 6–7.**

First line: "I heard only my labored breathing and the crunch of my crampons biting into snow as I traversed a nearly vertical slope on the north face of Mount Everest."

The pitch: When he was in fourth grade, Jordan Romero told his father that he had "decided to climb the highest peak on each of the seven continents: The Seven Summits." Jordan was inspired by a mural showing the Seven Summits in his elementary school hallway. He comes from a family of athletes who "compete in extreme adventure races all over the world." They are very supportive of his dream, even when he tells them he wants to climb "not when I'm older, but, like right now." Up to this point in his life, Jordan wasn't much of a hiker and his family hadn't climbed mountains, but as Jordan points out, "When I get interested in something, I become a fanatic and learn everything I can about it." They begin training right away, and one of the best pieces of advice he gets is to "take one small step at a time." Finally, Jordan is ready for his first summit—Mount Kilimanjaro in Africa.

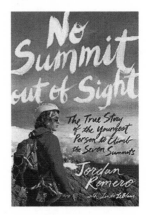

Reading selection: Read the second half of chapter 7, beginning with the line: "We walked single file up a path that got steeper and steeper, with endless switchbacks going up, up, up on mounds of small loose rocks called scree." When they reach eighteen thousand feet, ten-year-old Jordan "hit a wall" and couldn't continue. His guide Samuel tells him, "You're the strongest kid I've ever seen. You're going at an unbelievable pace. I'm extremely proud to be your guide." Samuel goes on by saying, "The mountain wants you to climb it." Jordan makes it to the summit at 19,341 feet. The chapter ends with Jordan claiming, "It was the craziest feeling I'd ever experienced."

Read-alike recommendation: Peak by Roland Smith (Harcourt, 2007) is a fictional account of a fourteen-year-old boy whose father is pushing him to become the youngest climber to summit Mount Everest.

Schatz, Kate. *Rad American Women A–Z*. City Lights, 2015. Gr. 5–7.

First line: "Angela Davis was born in 1944 in Birmingham, Alabama, into a neighborhood known as 'Dynamite Hill' because a group of racist white men called the Ku Klux Klan often bombed the homes of black families who lived there."

The pitch: That's the start of a one-page biography of activist and author Angela Davis, who fought "against racism and sexism, and in favor of gay rights," and who represents the letter "A" in this biography collection of "rad/radical" women. There's Billie Jean King, a professional tennis player who fought against sexism, "C" for Carol Burnett, a television comedian and pioneer, all the way to Zora Neale Hurston, an author who wrote about black culture, for the letter "Z." We learn about women who helped shape the civil rights movement (Ella Baker), abolitionists (the Grimke sisters), musicians (Hazel Scott), dancers (Isadora Duncan), airplane pilots (Queen Bessie Coleman), and more. Which woman represents the letter "X"? They don't have one. Instead, the letter "X" represents all the women throughout history whose names we don't know, whose voices weren't heard, or whose "radical histories" didn't get recorded. Check out the woman who represents the letter "J."

Reading selection: Read the entry for "J Is for Jovita," the story of Jovita Idar, journalist and teacher who fought for the right of Mexican American children to receive proper educational support. Jovita's father owned a newspaper "that published articles in Spanish, many of which spoke out against the prejudice experienced by the Idars and many other families who were Mexican and Te-jano (Texans of Spanish or Mexican heritage)." Jovita also wrote an article that criticized President Woodrow Wilson. The Texas Rangers tried to shut down the newspaper after it was printed. "Jovita stood in the doorway to block them from entering and to defend her freedom of speech."

Read-alike recommendation: Bad Girls: Sirens, Jezebels, Murderesses, Thieves & Other Female Villains by Jane Yolen and Heidi E. Y. Stemple (Charlesbridge, 2013) is another collection of short biographies of strong-willed women.

Scieszka, Jon. *Knucklehead: Tall Tales & Mostly True Stories of Growing Up Scieszka.* Viking, 2008. Gr. 3–6.

First line: "I grew up in Flint, Michigan, with my five brothers—Jim, Tom, Gregg, Brian, and What's-His-Name."

The pitch: What's-His-Name is Jon Scieszka's brother Jeff, the youngest of six boys. If Jon Scieszka's name sounds familiar, he's the guy who wrote *The Stinky Cheeseman and Other Fairly Stupid Tales* book, the Time Warp Trio series, and a lot more. Very funny books. He says that his ideas mostly came from "all the strange things that happened to me growing up with five brothers." Once, he and his older brothers saw Jeff pick up a cigarette butt, chew on it, and spit it out. They gave Jeff another butt and he did it again. They charged their friends ten cents to watch their little brother chew on cigarette butts. Another time, while playing "Slaughter Ball," their name for football, Gregg broke his collarbone. Jon and his brothers brought Gregg home and told their mother, "Sorry, Mom. We broke Gregg." Gregg and the other siblings kept "breaking" while playing other games like Jam Pile, Swing Jump, and Bicycle Demolition Derby. Here are other incidents that helped Jon become a funny guy.

Reading selection: Read chapter 16, "Brother-Sitting." Jon's parents worked, and so the older boys often watched the younger brothers. When Tom didn't stay in his bed, Jon and Jim "tied him up. In his bed. With my dad's ties." Their mother was hysterical when she found out. She asked them what might have happened if there were a fire. "'It would have burned off the ties,' said Jim. 'Then Tom could have escaped,' I added." On those occasions when they did have an "outside" babysitter, a neighbor girl, the boys proved to be a challenge.

One babysitter let the boys tie her up in the closet while playing Cowboys and Indians. She never came back. The chapter concludes with Jon musing, "We were never sure why. But now I realize that two hours tied up in a closet might have been just a little too long."

Read-alike recommendation: Guy-Write: What Every Guy Writer Needs to Know by Ralph J. Fletcher (Holt, 2012) has advice for boys on how to write as well as advice from writers like Jon Scieszka.

CHAPTER 12

Novels-in-Verse

While some reluctant readers might balk at the notion of reading poetry, novels-in-verse, stories made up of connective poems to tell one long story, are surprisingly popular with kids struggling to read. There is usually a lot of white space and short lines that make the reader flip through the book at a faster pace than a traditional prose book. They will quickly learn to adjust to the line breaks (represented here by "/") and go with the flow of the narrative by following traditional punctuation.

Bauer, Marion Dane. *Little Cat's Luck.* **Simon & Schuster, 2016. Gr. 3–5.**
  First lines: "Little cat, / searching. / Little calico cat / searching for a place, / a special place / to be her very own."
  The pitch: Patches, a house cat, is looking for a special place "hidden away / snug / dark, / quiet . . . / very, very quiet." One day, the window screen gives way and Patches finds herself in the "BIG world." She's not frightened, even though, perhaps, she should be. "The truth was / she knew as much / about / living outside / on her own / as you and I would know / about living / on the moon." She encounters a large, smelly, mean dog named Gus, who barks at cars, bicycles, joggers, and even birds. He shows everyone he's the boss by curling his lips, growling, snarling, and yelling, "GO! / Get out of here! / Go! Go! Go!"
  Reading selection: Read chapter 6. Gus is surprised to learn Patches isn't afraid of him. He barks, "Get out of my sight / you ugly thing!" Patches still doesn't run away. Gus has a reputation as the meanest dog in town, and he roars at her to leave "THIS INSTANT!" Patches flips her tail at Gus, so once again he barks, "GO! GO! GO! / And don't you / ever, / ever, / ever / come back!" Before she leaves, Patches notices Gus's food and dish bowls. The chapter ends with the lines: "This / was a place / to remember. / After all, / the great noisy thing / had to sleep / sometime. / Didn't he?"

Read-alike recommendation: Author Bauer also wrote a companion novel-in-verse titled *Little Dog Lost* (2012), the story of a boy who needs a dog and a dog who needs a boy.

Bingham, Kelly. *Shark Girl.* Candlewick, 2007. Gr. 6–7.

First lines: "Sometimes / I can still feel my right hand, / like a best friend; / weighted, / warm."

The pitch: Fifteen-year-old Jane was attacked by a shark just a few yards from shore. Her brother Michael helped save her life by taking the cord from his swimsuit and tying it on the limb to prevent more blood loss. A man on the beach recorded the whole thing, and the news stations played it over and over for weeks. Jane learns about all this when she wakes up from a coma ten weeks after the attack. Her right arm needed to be amputated above the elbow. Jane was an award-winning artist. How will she draw now? How will she cope when she leaves the hospital? She thinks, "Missing an arm is like wearing a coat, / a really big, hot, ugly coat / that I can't take off. / Ever. / It's all that people see." After her long hospital stay, and after being at home to recuperate, she's not sure she's ready to return to school.

Reading selection: Read a series of poems from part 2, beginning with the poem titled "Lighted Numbers." Jane is awake the night before going back to school, staring at her clock. She thinks, "I'd rather go back / to that beach / and dip my toes / in the cold gray water, / than step into school / in just a few hours." Read the next two poems, "Drowning" and "Current." Jane is aware of people staring at her. The next poem, "Whispers," consists of the dialogue of students talking about Jane. "That girl that got bitten by a . . . and then the shark just . . . ?" Skip the poem "I Could Run Away, but Then What?" and read "Shark Girl." Jane once again overhears students talking about her. Skip the poems "Art Class" and "The Hallway Encounter That Leaves Me Weak in the Knees" and finish the selection with "Crap Overheard," another poem filled with other student comments. It ends with the lines: "I want to talk to her, you know? Say something But I / don't know what." / "She would probably rather be left alone, anyway." / "Yeah. Probably."

Read-alike recommendations: Jane's story continues in the sequel *Formerly Shark Girl* (2013) where she is now a high school senior. A similar real-life story can be found in the prose-style autobiography *Soul Surfer: A True Story of Faith, Family, and Fighting to Get Back on the Board* by Bethany Hamilton (Pocket,

2004). Bethany lost her left arm when she was thirteen years old and went on to compete as a surfer.

Engle, Margarita. *Mountain Dog.* **Holt, 2013. Gr. 4–7.**

First lines: "In my other life there were pit bulls. / The puppies weren't born vicious, / but Mom taught them how to bite, / turning meanness into money, / until she got caught."

The pitch: Tony's mother raises pit bulls to fight each other, which is, of course, illegal. When she is sent to prison, Tony is sent to live with his uncle Tio, who lives on a mountain as a park ranger. Tio is often called to help locate missing hikers and hunters in the woods, always with his rescue dog Gabe. It doesn't take Tony long to embrace his new home and bond with Gabe. Tony learns that, like himself, Gabe has been rescued from a rough life and now has a new purpose: to help find lost people and save their lives. Tony, the city kid learning about the woods, and the chocolate lab Gabe take turns telling the story. One day, Tony goes down the mountain with Tio and Gabe to visit his mother in prison. He is upset because she refuses to see him. On the way back up to their mountain home, Tio gets a call. A little girl, three years old, is lost in the woods. . . .

Reading selection: Read the second half of chapter 7, beginning with the lines: "So we drive to a farm / where volunteers gather / around a sheriff, listening / to instructions." Gabe is wearing a vest covered with light sticks, and "he streaks / through the darkness / of night / making light / seem like something alive / and growing. . . ." Tony doesn't follow his uncle's instructions to stay put and joins the search. End that chapter and read the short chapter 8, "Hide-and-Seek." Gabe doesn't understand why humans cannot pick up scents like dogs. Skip ahead to chapter 13, "Loser." Tony finally visits his mother and notices that she has new tattoos of paw prints for "each fighting pit bull / that ever won a battle" and teardrops for "each dog / that lost its life." The chapter ends with Tony leaving his mother. "I come away from those visits / feeling like such a loser. / If I turned into a tattoo / on Mom's face, / I'd be / a teardrop."

Read-alike recommendations: Diamond Willow by Helen Frost (Farrar Straus Giroux, 2008) is composed of diamond-shaped poems that tell of a girl named Willow who goes on a dogsled trip in Alaska. *Ellie's Story: A Dog's Purpose Novel* by W. Bruce Cameron (Starscape, 2015) is a non-verse story of a rescue dog named Ellie who tells her own story about being trained to track down lost people.

Frost, Helen. *Hidden.* **Frances Foster, 2011. Gr. 5–7.**

First lines: "I was a happy little girl wearing a pink dress, / sitting in our gold minivan, / dancing with my doll, Kamara."

The pitch: Wren's happiness disappears when she hears a gunshot and a strange man steals her car with Wren in the backseat. She hides "like a small rabbit / that knows a cat is close by, / I paid attention. I didn't / twitch." The man parks the minivan in his garage. Wren hears a woman shouting that the kidnapping made the news. "*This is the car they're searching for! / What happened / to Wren Abbott?*" The man and woman fight and enter the house. The two have a daughter named Darra who suspects Wren might be in the garage. She calls out, "*Stay out here tonight. / He won't hurt you if you stay out of his way. / I bet you're hungry. Here's some food and water. /* The door closed." Wren is hiding in a boat stored in the garage and overhears the man planning to dump the minivan at a mall while his wife and Darra follow in their truck. As the garage door comes down, Wren rolls under it.

Reading selection: Begin reading poem 35 of part 1: "A huge white dog / lunged at me. / Growling." Wren rolls back under the garage door before it shuts all the way. She's still trapped in the garage. A cat named Archie keeps her company, even dropping a dead mouse in her lap. When a skunk gets into the garage, Wren finds a pet door hidden in the corner of the garage. "(Could I fit through? What if I get stuck halfway?) / (Where is the dog? Is it chained?)" She twists her body through the door. The dog sees her and growls. End the reading with the following lines: "The skunk lifted its tail. The dog yelped, / and I ran—past the skunk, past the dog, / down the long driveway, in one shoe / and the big gray sweatshirt. / Clutching Kamara like life itself. / Leaving Archie / and Darra / behind."

Read-alike recommendation: The Wild Book by Margarita Engle (Harcourt, 2012) is a novel-in-verse set in 1912 Cuba and features Fefa, a dyslexic girl living in a land where roaming bandits kidnap children for ransom.

Holt, K. A. *Rhyme Schemer*. Chronicle, 2014. Gr. 5–7.

First lines: "First day of school. / My favorite. / Easy prey."

The pitch: We're in seventh grader Kevin's head. He is an angry kid who picks on several other kids at school, particularly a small boy named Robin. Kevin calls himself a stone. He is very judgmental about his teachers and principal. Kevin calls the mole on Mrs. Smithson's face Harry. Kevin keeps a notebook and he writes, "Harry gives a shake / when Mrs. Smithson / sneezes / turns her head / walks too fast / laughs / hollers." Kevin starts ripping pages out of library books and scribbles on them, creating little messages. He posts them on the school walls and writes they are from "a secret word scrambler." Kevin's older brother Petey dislikes his younger brother and throws Kevin's notebook out of the car one day, yelling, "Poetry is for old ladies." Kevin catches Robin bullying another kid and drags him into the boys' bathroom. He is caught stuffing Robin "between the pipes / like a Lego / like he was made to fit there." Kevin is suspended from school for three days.

Reading selection: Read a series of Kevin's poems starting with Day 19. Kevin is mad because people are upset he shoved Robin under the sinks, but no one cares when "Petey shoves me under the sink / in the bathroom at home / All. / The. / Time." Robin finds Kevin's notebook, and that bothers Kevin. His secret love of poetry is in danger of being exposed. "No one can hear your heart beat fast / when you are jagged stone." Finish the reading with the first part of Day 24. Robin makes copies of Kevin's notebook. End the passage with the lines: "Guess who's going to get to watch his nose / EXPLODE OFF HIS FACE?"

Read-alike recommendation: Falling into the Dragon's Mouth by Holly Thompson (Holt, 2016) is a novel-in-verse story of an American boy bullied in his new home in Japan.

Rose, Caroline Starr. *May B.* Schwartz & Wade, 2012. Gr. 4–7.

First line: "I won't go."

The pitch: It's the 1800s on the Kansas prairie. May has been ordered by her parents to work for the Oblingers, a young married couple who live fifteen miles from May's home. May's salary will help her own family. She has trouble reading in school and worries she'll fall further behind her classmates. She plays with the words in her name: "Maybe May B. can / Maybe May B. can't." Her full name is Mavis Elizabeth Betterly. She shortens it to May Betts, and again to May B. She is told she'll sleep in the corner of the Oblingers' sod house. "A dingy corner, / muslin pinned across the ceiling / stained brown / from rain that seeps through the sod." When Mrs. Oblinger catches May looking at the ceiling, she says, "You'll be no wetter than the rest of us." May overhears Mrs. Oblinger mutter, "Stupid girl." Mrs. Oblinger later confesses that she was wrong to live on the prairie. "But his letter was so kind. / I didn't think through prairie living." Mrs. Oblinger leaves for Ohio.

Reading selection: Start reading poem 41. Mr. Oblinger hitches the wagon and goes after his wife. He tells May not to worry about supper. "I could be gone some time." Continue reading poems 41 through 52. For the first time in her life, May is completely alone. She gets things ready for the couple's return. When they don't come back, May worries. "I dread the blackness / growing stronger outside." She hears strange noises at night. "Gooseflesh ripples / up my arms. / I squeeze my knees tighter. / When / will morning / come?" By the fourth day, May realizes that something's very, very wrong. She looks at the surrounding land. "There is nothing here to mark my place, / nothing to show me where I am." The last poem of this section ends with the lines: "Pa doesn't know they won't return / The nearest neighbor is gone. / I'm here till Christmas."

Read-alike recommendation: Cabin on Trouble Creek by Jean Van Leeuwen (Dial, 2004) is set in 1803 and features two brothers alone in the woods when their father goes back east to fetch the rest of the family.

Wissinger, Tamara Will. *Gone Fishing.* **Houghton Mifflin Harcourt, 2013. Gr. 3–5.**

First lines: "Dark night. / Flashlight. / Dad and I hunt worms tonight."

The pitch: Sam is looking forward to a fishing trip with his dad. Just the two of them. They find ninety-four night crawlers the night before the trip. Sam checks his tackle box and looks at "my silver sinkers, wiggle worms, my floating frogs, my line. / My shiny spinner lures, my bobbers, hooks—there're twenty-nine." He keeps inspecting and is surprised to find a princess doll in his tackle box. "I smell *Lucy* in the room." Lucy is his little sister, the last person he wants to hang around. He wishes a fishy curse spell on her: "May a worm crawl up your nose, / Leeches creep between your toes. / May your nails be caked with dirt. / May a bug fly up your skirt." Lucy convinces their father to take her along on the fishing trip. They take forever to leave because Lucy is the "slowpoke of the year." To make matters worse, Lucy starts catching fish and all Sam has caught is an old cap.

Reading selection: Read the poem titled "Lucy's Song." Lucy sings an annoying song while they are sitting in the boat. "Heeere, fishy, fishy, fishy. / Tasty worms for lunch today. / Heeere, fishy, fishy, fish." After Lucy catches a fish, her envious brother sings her song. "*Heeere, fishy, fishy, fishy. / I repeat it quietly. / Heeerre, fishy, fishy, fish. / It worked for Lucy—why not me?*" Next, read the poem "Fishing Score." Lucy has caught eight fish and Sam has caught none. Sam complains that she's using up all the bait. Finish by reading the poem titled "Gulp." Lucy is proud that Sam finally caught a fish. Sam feels ashamed that he didn't even look at her when she caught her first fish. The poem ends with Sam thinking, "Maybe I was wrong / about bringing her along."

Read-alike recommendation: Toasting Marshmallows by Kristine O'Connell George (Clarion, 2001) is a collection of short poems about all aspects of camping, from pitching a tent to observing wildlife. One poem features the narrator's dog dreaming of becoming a timber wolf.

Zimmer, Tracie Vaughn. *42 Miles.* **Clarion, 2008. Gr. 4–6.**

First line: "Until this year / my parents lived / four blocks apart / in Cincinnati."

The pitch: Now, twelve-year-old JoEllen spends "school days in the city with Mom / weekends on the farm with Dad / holidays, birthday, summer vacation— / all negotiated." Forty-two miles apart. Two different lifestyles. Two identities.

JoEllen says, "Now my days— / divided between them— / are as different as my names." When she's with her father and her rural relatives, she goes by Joey. With mom and classmates, she's Ellen. At the farm, she spends a lot of time with her cousin Hayden. At school in the city, her best friends are Annie and Tamika and her enemy is Belinda. JoEllen tells us about all of them. For example, Annie is a big scaredy-cat, worried about things like Lyme disease and the additives in the school food. "But she can take down / a two-hundred-pound man / in judo class." As JoEllen tries to figure out her life, she gets a dreaded assignment in school.

Reading selection: Read the poem "Autobiography." JoEllen's teacher instructs the students to write their autobiography. JoEllen doesn't know if she should write about being Joey or about her life as Ellen. She says, "This assignment / makes running the seven-minute mile / in gym class / seem painless by comparison." Skip to the poem "Toes." In the girls' bathroom, Belinda insults Tamika by calling her the Trash Queen. JoEllen finds the courage to confront the bully by stepping on her toes and saying, "Don't Ever. Call her that. Again." Continue reading "Empty Spaces." Tamika and Annie don't know anything about country life and Hayden, in turn, doesn't know much about city life, "listening to street music / wearing vintage fashions / working at the secondhand store." Next, read "Questions." JoEllen wonders if she can risk a zero if she doesn't write her autobiography. Skip to "Thirteen" and finish with this poem. JoEllen is about to turn thirteen and she has decided that "my two lives / are going to meet / and shake hands." She wants everyone to call her JoEllen. The poem ends with the sentence: "And this is just / the beginning."

Read-alike-recommendations: Locomotion by Jacqueline Woodson (Putnam, 2003) is about Lonnie, nicknamed "Locomotion," who is trying to learn who he is after his parents died in a fire. The sequel is *Peace, Locomotion* (2009).

CHAPTER 13

Friends and Family

For many reluctant readers, the books they eventually turn to are the books they can relate to. Books where aspects of friendship or family members (the two groups often combine in many stories) are one of the main focuses of the story have been compiled in this section.

Acampora, Paul. *Rachel Spinelli Punched Me in the Face.* **Roaring Brook, 2011. Gr. 5–7.**

First line: "For several days, after Dad and I discovered that Mom had gone, we tried very hard to lie."

The pitch: The truth is that Zachary and his father have to move on after his mother leaves them. They literally move to a new town. The very first person Zachary meets is his new neighbor Rachel Spinelli, who has a reputation for being hotheaded. She is very defensive about her older brother Teddy, a tall musical genius who doesn't always follow social norms. For example, on the very first day of summer vacation when kids are looking forward to sleeping in late, Teddy arrives at Zachary's house at 5:30 in the morning and plays "'Call to the Post.' That's the tune they play at the race tracks just before the announcer yells, 'THEY'RE OFF!!'" And if you were paying attention to the title of this book, yes, somewhere in the story, Rachel hauls off and punches Zachary. Gives him a black eye. Before that happens, though, here's a little taste of that infamous Rachel Spinelli temper.

Reading selection: Read chapter 5. Zachary runs into Rachel in the school cafeteria. They notice Mike Kutzler, the "football alpha dog," giving Teddy a hard time. When Zachary yells at Mike to leave Teddy alone, Mike says, "I've got one retard in front of me and another one behind me." That sets Rachel off. She calls Mike an idiot and slaps his lunch tray out of his hands. When the cafeteria monitor "who happened to be Mr. Behr, the Falls High School football coach," comes over to check on the commotion, Mike whines that Rachel has to pay for his lunch. "Without warning, she tipped her own lunch tray forward. A slice of pizza and an extra tall cup of ice tea poured onto Mike Kutzler's pants like a science experiment gone bad." When Rachel asks the coach if she'll have detention, he replies, "After school wouldn't be the same without you." The chapter ends with Zachary noting that Rachel's superpower is her protection of Teddy.

Read-alike recommendation: Because of Winn-Dixie by Kate DiCamillo (Candlewick, 2000) has some of the same elements as *Rachel Spinelli Punched Me in the Face.* A girl named Opal moves to a new small town with her father, finds a dog in a grocery store, and slowly meets the slightly eccentric townspeople.

Barrows, Annie. *Ivy + Bean Break the Fossil Record.* Chronicle, 2007. Gr. 3–4.

First lines: "Boring. Boring! **Boring!**"

The pitch: Bean is not enjoying the book she chose for her classroom's Drop Everything and Read program. Her friend Ivy and all the other kids are engrossed in their own books. "Ivy's eyes were binging across the pages of her book. Bing, bing, bing. She looked like she was watching a Ping-Pong game." Their teacher gives Bean *The Amazing Book of World Records.* Bean is fascinated by the man who ate thirty scorpions in one day, the kid with 256 straws in his mouth, and the lady who broke glass by screaming. She is feeling "unfamous and unimportant" and decides to break some world records of her own. First, she tries to fit 257 straws in her mouth with help from Ivy but she can't fit more than forty-seven. Next, she tries to break her sister's glass octopus by screaming, but that only makes her sister angry. She and Ivy decide they will become the world's youngest paleontologists. The two dig up twenty-one dinosaur bones in Bean's backyard and invite all the kids in school over to see their discovery.

Reading selection: Read the chapter titled "Dorkosaurus." The girls are putting the bones together and both start singing. "Oh, the neck bone's connected to the shoulder bone. . . . " Bean's older sister Nancy comes in and calls their dinosaur a "dorkosaurus." She tells them the people who lived in their house before them owned a dog that buried the bones. "'Look'—she pointed at the neck bone—'That's a steak bone.'" Bean's father tries to comfort the sad girls. The chapter ends with the lines: "There was a knock on the backyard gate. 'Who's that?' asked Bean's dad. 'Everybody,' said Ivy glumly."

Read-alike recommendations: This is the third book about Ivy and Bean. The other titles are *Ivy + Bean* (2006), *Ivy + Bean and the Ghost That Had to Go* (2006), *Ivy + Bean Take Care of the Babysitter* (2008), *Ivy + Bean: Bound to Be Bad* (2008), *Ivy + Bean: Doomed to Dance* (2009), *Ivy + Bean: What's the Big Idea?* (2010), *Ivy + Bean: No News Is Good News* (2011), *Ivy + Bean Make the Rules* (2012), and *Ivy + Bean Take the Case* (2013).

Bonder-Stone, Annabeth, and Connor White. *Shivers! The Pirate Who's Afraid of Everything.* **Harper, 2015. Gr. 3–5.**
  First line: "BEEP-BEEP! BEEP-BEEP!"
  The pitch: Shivers is the name of a kid pirate and he has just jumped out of bed, convinced the alarm sound he hears means danger. He starts to put his Emergency Attack Plan into operation, first by putting on his helmet, and then reinforcing the fort walls and preparing for a hurricane or alien attack. "Shivers cowered in the corner next to his bed and realized what was really making the sound. 'MY ALARM CLOCK!' he shouted." He bravely turns the snooze button off. Shivers lives on a beached pirate ship. He's too nervous to actually go out on the water. He is named Shivers because he is always "shaking and shivering in a corner." His parents and brother are famous pirates. His mother is known as Tilda the Tormentor because "she once tied up and taunted an entire army of vicious sea creatures without coming up for air." A carrier pigeon frightens Shivers before dropping off a note that his parents and brother have been captured and are prisoners somewhere. Shivers goes to the local police station for help and runs into the police chief's daughter Margo, who loves adventure.
  Reading selection: Read a few pages into chapter 2, with the line: "'A pirate!' Margo shouted." Her father sighs when he sees Shivers. Apparently, in the past, Shivers has asked the police to clear the dust out of his closet because it looked like poisonous spiders and to remove snails from the daisies. The police have also had to tell Shivers not to worry about the bathwater. "The water is *supposed* to disappear after you take a bath." Margo brags about her bravery. "Why, I've tied up kidnappers and locked them up to rot. I've tracked down the world's darkest evildoers, and when I was finished with them, they were evil-undoers. And that was just this weekend." When she hears that Shivers's family has been captured, she says, "'Well, let's go find them!'" End the reading with the next sentence: "She started to wave her stick above her head like a sword."
  Read-alike recommendations: Shivers and Margo return in *Shivers! The Pirate Who's Back in Bunny Slippers* (2016). Another humorous pirate-family book is *Uncle Pirate* by Douglas Reese (Margaret K. McElderry, 2008) and its sequel *Uncle Pirate to the Rescue* (2010). Wilson's long-lost uncle and his penguin come to live with Wilson's family.

Gephart, Donna. *Death by Toilet Paper.* **Delacorte, 2014. Gr. 4–7.**

First lines: "Dear Royal—T Toilet Paper Company, You guys make the best toilet paper on the planet. I realize that's a weird thing for a seventh grader to say, but it's true."

The pitch: The reason Ben is writing to a toilet paper company is because, ever since his father died, he and his mother are struggling to make ends meet. He sometimes steals toilet paper because his mother buys the cheapest recycled brand they can afford. He complains, "The stuff's so rough, I'd be better off wiping my butt with tree bark." Ben even throws in some fun facts about toilet paper and toilets throughout his story, little bits of information such as toilet paper wasn't around in the Middle Ages. "Rich people used wool or hemp. Poor people were stuck using stones, mussel shells or grass." The real reason Ben is in touch with the toilet paper company is that he's trying to win a contest. First prize is $10,000. Ben wants the money to save them from being evicted. Ben is sensitive about their money problems, even when he hangs out with his best friend Toothpick. Yup, the guy's nickname is Toothpick.

Reading selection: Read the opening chapter that begins after the first letter to the toilet paper company. The selection opens with the lines: "Blood spatters cover every surface—the kitchen table, including the pepper mill, the wall behind the table and much of the tile floor. Even their cat, Psycho, has a blood splatter across her white fur." The blood is actually salsa and Toothpick and Ben are making a horror movie titled *Guess Who We're Having for Dinner.* Toothpick's father makes an extra pan of lasagna and insists Ben take it home. Ben does not want to hurt his feelings but doesn't want to take a handout, either. "*Things will get better,* I tell myself, *because I will make them better.*" Before Ben goes home, he says, "That's how I spend my Saturday afternoon: doing fierce battle with a skittish, salsa-spattered cat, cleaning up after a bloody murder scene and taking toilet paper from my best friend's bathroom." But he won't take the lasagna.

Read-alike recommendation: How to Steal a Dog by Barbara O'Connor (Farrar Straus Giroux, 2007) features a girl named Georgina who comes up with a moneymaking scheme for her family's homeless situation. She's going to steal a dog and then claim the reward money.

Green, D. L. *Zeke Meeks vs. the Annoying Princess Sing-Along.* **Picture Window, 2015. Gr. 3–4.**

First lines: "Ugh! My little sister was watching the *Princess Sing-Along* TV show."

The pitch: The *Princess Sing-Along* show is for little girls like Zeke's sister Mia. The star of the show and her many young followers sing message songs like, "Don't pet any dogs that you don't know, la la la. They could grab your hand and not let go, la la la. Once your hand becomes entangled, la la la, it could get bloody and mangled, la la la." Zeke's older sister is listening to the band Young Hot Dudes in another room. Their poor dog Waggles is dressed up in a Beauty Queen T-shirt. Zeke moans that he is "so tired of my sisters and their girly stuff." Zeke says he likes school "except for math, reading, writing, science, history, geography, worksheets, reports, tests, studying, learning, and listening to my teacher." That leaves lunch, recess, "and leaving." His teacher Mr. McNutty assigns them to report on what they are going to do over the weekend. Zeke had other plans but, because his little sister's friends got sick, he agrees to join her for the Princess Sing-Along concert.

Reading selection: Read chapter 5, "A Shocking Sight." Zeke, his family, and his friend Hector, whom he convinced to join him, get to the concert hall. Zeke's mother complains about the price of parking. The boys hope no one they know sees them. Hector points and says, "Luh mih McNuhnuh." It's their teacher Mr. McNutty with his daughter. Once inside, Zeke's mother complains about the price of the program and also the drinks. A little girl behind Zeke kicks his chair and asks her father when will the show start. The father is holding a crying baby. Zeke is surrounded by excited preschool-age girls. The chapter ends with the lines: "The girl kicked my chair again. The baby kept crying. The little girls in the audience screamed. I screamed silently to myself: *I'm already sick of this horrible concert!*"

Read-alike recommendations: There are many more books about Zeke and his family, including *Zeke Meeks vs. the Gruesome Girls* (2012), *Zeke Meeks vs. the Horrible TV-Turnoff Week* (2012), *Zeke Meeks vs. the Putrid Puppet Pals* (2012), *Zeke Meeks vs. the Stinkin' Science Fair* (2012), *Zeke Meeks vs. the Big Blah-rific Birthday* (2013), *Zeke Meeks vs. the Horrendous Halloween* (2013), *Zeke Meeks vs. the Super Stressful Talent Show* (2013), *Zeke Meeks vs. the No-Fun Fund-Raiser* (2013), *Zeke Meeks vs. His Big Phony Cousin* (2014), *Zeke Meeks vs. the Pain-in-the-Neck Pets* (2014), *Zeke Meeks vs. the Crummy Class Play* (2014), *Zeke Meeks vs. the Mother's Day Meltdown* (2015), and *Zeke Meeks vs. the Stinky Soccer Team* (2015).

Hanlon, Abby. *Dory Fantasmagory*. Dial, 2014. Gr. 3–4.

First line: "My name is Dory, but everyone calls me Rascal."

The pitch: Dory, or Rascal as her family calls her, is one of those kids who doesn't know when to stop being a pest. Her older siblings Violet and Luke complain about every single thing she does. They say, "She's looking at us" and "She's breathing." Violet and Luke decide to scare Dory by making up an imaginary person named Mrs. Gobble Gracker. They tell her, "Mrs. Gobble Gracker is a robber, and she steals baby girls." Their plan backfires when Dory becomes excited about the idea of Mrs. Gobble Gracker. She pesters them with more questions. "Is she sneaky? Will I have to battle her? Does she wear a long black cape? Is it made out of fur? Is it real fur or fake fur? Are her teeth rotting? Does she brush them? Does she have a really creepy-looking nose? Does she have a cat? Does she live in a cave? Does she really have long bones?" Dory pretends to knock out Mrs. Gobble Gracker by sticking a sleeping dart in her butt. With that out of her way, she once again turns her attention to her older brother and sister.

Reading selection: Read the first part of chapter 3, "Chickenbone." Dory puts on her cow costume and bugs Violet and Luke. She shows them a magic trick. "'See the stick in this hand?' I say. Then I put my hands behind my back. 'Now it's in this hand. Ta-da!' 'That's the worst trick I've ever seen,' says Luke." She gets mad when they tell her she's acting like a baby, and she gets even madder when her mother demands she takes off her cow costume. End the selection when Dory says, "I unbutton my cow costume and strip down to my underwear because *it's way too hot to have this temper tantrum in a cow costume . . .* **not** because they told me to!"

Read-alike recommendations: Dory returns in *Dory and the Real True Friend* (2015) and *Dory Dory Black Sheep* (2016). Another fun series featuring a pesky younger sibling is the Stink series by Megan McDonald. The titles are *Stink: The Incredible Shrinking Kid* (Candlewick, 2005), *Stink and the Incredible, Super-Galactic Jawbreaker* (2006), *Stink and the World's Worst Super-Stinky Sneakers* (2007), *Stink and the Great Guinea Pig Express* (2008), *Stink: Solar System Superhero* (2010), *Stink and the Ultimate Thumb-Wrestling Smackdown* (2011), *Stink and the Midnight Zombie Walk* (2012), *Stink and the Freaky Frog Freakout* (2013), and *Stink and the Shark Sleepover* (2014).

Marshall III, Joseph. *In the Footsteps of Crazy Horse.* Amulet, 2015. Gr. 4–6.

First lines: "Jimmy McClean walked among the buffalo berry thickets along the Smoking Earth River. It was a warm afternoon in late May. School was done for the week, and almost for the year. Jimmy was glad of that. He was tired of being teased for having blue eyes."

The pitch: Jimmy lives on the Rosebud Sioux Indian Reservation and he is picked on by both a white kid and a Lakota kid. Corky, the white kid, says, "You're just an Indian pretending to be white," while the Lakota kid Jesse teases, "Who ever heard of a Lakota with blue eyes and a name like McClean?" Jimmy had been told by his mother "that three parts of Jimmy were Lakota and one part was white. That part was Scottish, to be exact. The problem is your three Lakota parts are all hidden inside." Jimmy's grandfather Nyles explains that the great figure Crazy Horse was also teased for having light skin and brown hair. Jimmy and his grandfather go on a summer journey through four states to learn more about Crazy Horse and Jimmy's own Lakota heritage. Grandfather Nyles shares many stories including one where Crazy Horse devised a plan to fool white soldiers, known as Long Knives. He copied the ways of a mother grouse who acted wounded to lead coyotes away from her nest. Crazy Horse and his companions appeared vulnerable in order to draw the Long Knives into a trap.

Reading selection: Read the last fourth of chapter 4, "The Bozeman Trail," beginning with the line: "Crazy Horse and his decoys turned their horses back to the north." Grandfather shares the story of how Crazy Horse's flanking maneuver turned into victory for the Lakota warriors. At the end of the story, Grandfather Nyles mentions that around forty warriors were killed and all eighty Long Knives lost their lives. "We should never forget them and what happened here. But we have to remember the soldiers kindly, too." End the passage short of the chapter's end with Grandfather Nyles saying this about Crazy Horse: "He didn't want to be a leader. He just wanted to be a good man and a good warrior."

Read-alike recommendation: Author Marshall also contributed to the book project titled *Walking on Earth & Touching the Sky: Poetry and Prose by Lakota Youth at Red Cloud Indian School*, edited by Timothy B. McLaughlin (Abrams, 2012).

Narsimhan, Mahtab. *Mission Mumbai: A Novel of Sacred Cows, Snakes, and Stolen Toilets.* Scholastic, 2016. Gr. 4–7.

First line: "I wanted a clear shot but there were too many people blocking the way."

The pitch: Twelve-year-old Dylan from New York didn't realize that hitting a cow with a stick in India would result in a mob chasing him. He didn't actually hit the cow hard. He smacked it on its backside and it "jumped up with a plaintive moo." It was enough to make the locals very angry. Dylan is on a trip to India with his best friend Rohit and Rohit's mother Mrs. Lal, both who currently live in the United States but are back in their homeland to attend a wedding. After saving Dylan from the mob, she yells at him, "When you hit a cow, it is as if you're slapping one of their mothers. It is considered a huge insult." She then turns to her son. "This is the *first* time he's visiting India and you let him *hit a cow*?" Dylan and Rohit have been the best of friends. They are "nerds of a feather." They compare themselves to Sam and Frodo from the *Lord of the Rings* trilogy. Lately, though, their friendship is falling apart. Dylan wonders what other "trouble could a street-smart New Yorker get into in Mumbai?" Dylan, Rohit, and Rohit's parents are in a movie theater when the power goes out. Then, someone yells out, "Fire!"

Reading selection: Read chapter 16. Everyone runs to the exits. Dylan falls, and Rohit returns and helps him back on his feet. They make it outside of the theater and immediately start looking for Rohit's parents. "We wandered for another half hour, circling the theater, calling out their names, grabbing policemen and pedestrians, describing them till we were hoarse." Rohit starts blaming

Dylan. "If you hadn't insisted on watching a movie, we'd still be at home. Ma and Papa would have been safe and alive." The chapter ends with Dylan thinking, "I'd never felt so betrayed or utterly alone in my life."

Read-alike recommendation: Chloe in India by Kate Darnton (Delacorte, 2016) features an American girl moving from Boston to New Delhi and making friends with a girl named Lakshmi.

Neri, G. *Ghetto Cowboy*. Candlewick, 2011. Gr. 5–7.

First lines: "We drivin' into the sunset, the car burning up from the heat. I don't know if it's comin' from outside or from Mama, who's burning up angry at me."

The pitch: Twelve-year-old Cole's mama is burning mad because she just found out he's been skipping school for four weeks. Cole is very good at hiding letters and messages from the vice principal and ducking the truancy officer, partly because his mother is busy at work to support the two of them. But this is the last straw. Cole is suspended the last two weeks of class and will have to repeat seventh grade unless he goes to summer school. Cole panics when he realizes his mother is driving from their home in Detroit to Philadelphia. She's going to leave him with his father, a man he's never met.

Reading selection: Read chapter 3. Cole wakes up, realizing that his mother has driven through the night. They wind up on a run-down street when unexpectedly, a white horse runs by. Several people are chasing the horse. Mama stops and dumps Cole's belongings on the curb. Two "sleepy-eyed gangbangers" make fun of Cole's pleading. As Cole's mother drives away, the horse reappears and "BOOM! Mama's car sideswipes the horse. It hits the front of the car and the hood, then tumbles like a ton of bricks." Cole's father shows up with a gun in his hand. "I can tell it's him 'cause as soon as I see him walk onto the street, it's like I'm looking into the future or something. He looks exactly like me, only taller and older. And he definitely ain't in a good mood." The chapter ends with Cole's father sending his mother on her way and stepping up to the horse. Cole says, "The horse moans and groans, getting louder and louder until I hear the cock of the gun and a loud BANG! Then it's quiet again."

Read-alike recommendation: Ghetto Cowboy references the history of African American cowboys. The graphic novel biography *Best Shot in the West: The Adventures of Nat Love* by Patricia C. McKissack and Frederick L. McKissack (Chronicle, 2012) features one of the most notorious figures of the Wild West.

Reynolds, Jason. *As Brave as You.* Atheneum, 2016. Gr. 5–7.

First lines: "#460. POOP. POOP iS StuPid. StuPid POOP. StuPid. POOPid. POOPidity. IS POOPidity a WORd?"

The pitch: Genie and his older brother Ernie leave their Brooklyn home and spend a month in the Virginia country with their grandparents. One of his grandmother's rules is to help with chores and that means cleaning up after the dog. Ernie develops a system where he scoops up the dog poop and flings it into the woods. Genie wants to help. "No way was Genie going to miss out on slinging poop." They start aiming at specific trees and buildings. "We're talking technique here. Sophisticated stuff." Genie writes down questions and then looks up the answers on the Internet, questions like "How come teeth ain't called mouthnails? Or maybe fingernails should be called fingerteeth." Grandpop is blind but very independent. He has cages of birds named after the Jackson Five. Genie believes he accidentally killed the bird named Michael Jackson. He searches for a replacement bird. Genie and his brother head to an old building in the woods supposedly filled with birds.

Reading selection: Read the second half of chapter 12, beginning with the sentence: "Every so often, Genie turned around to see a) if there were any copperheads creeping up behind them, and b) how far they'd come." They are shocked at the condition of the house in the woods. "An old yellow house WITH A TREE GROWING UP THE CENTER OF IT. Holy moly—that tree had to be fifty feet high!" The brothers discover the house is indeed full of birds and bird mess. "They both pulled the necks of their T-shirts over their noses at exactly the same time. It wasn't funky. We're talking FOWNKY." When they don't catch a bird, Ernie has a fun idea. He slams a door and the birds explode into the air. Finish the reading with the line: "Just as the last bird had disappeared beyond the treetops, they heard Grandma's voice calling for them."

Read-alike recommendation: Lucky Strike by Bobbie Pyron (Arthur E. Levine, 2015) is another book featuring a boy and his grandfather. When unlucky Nate is struck by lightning, his bad luck changes to good luck.

CHAPTER 14

School

As in the case of the genres Friends and Family, stories set in schools are also a familiar aspect of a reluctant reader's life. Many of the stories included in this section feature humorous twists about the school experience or opportunities to learn about classmates who may be both somewhat similar or somewhat different from the reader.

Angleberger, Tom. *The Strange Case of Origami Yoda.* **Amulet, 2010. Gr. 4–7.**

First line: "The big question: Is Origami Yoda real?"

The pitch: Sixth grader Dwight is a clueless loser. During a school dance, he knocks over a girl's drink and then cleans up the spill by scotching "around on his stomach." To his friend's horror, Dwight stands back up with a stained shirt and starts dancing his "weird jumping-around thing" again. Dwight also

goes around with an origami finger puppet folded into the shape of Yoda from the Star Wars movies. He tells people to ask Origami Yoda for advice. When narrator Tommy thinks about dancing with Hannah, Origami Yoda (the puppet on Dwight's finger) says, "Rush in fools do." When Tommy hesitates, they all spot Hannah kissing a big hunky guy, thus saving Tommy from embarrassment. Is Origami Yoda real?

Reading selection: Read the chapter titled "Origami Yoda and the Embarrassing Stain." Kellen, one of Tommy's friends, gets water on his pants in the school bathroom. He's afraid that people will think he peed in his pants. "There was no way I could go to class with a giant pee stain! Which really wasn't pee." Dwight happens to be in the bathroom and Origami Yoda tells Kellen, "All of pants you must wet." Kellen soaks his pants and his shirt as well. When he returns to class, everyone wonders why he is all wet; nobody thinks he peed his pants. End the selection when Kellen says, "That's when I knew that Origami Yoda is for real, man! He's totally Jedi wise!"

Read-alike recommendations: The sequels include *Darth Paper Strikes Back* (2011), *The Secret of the Fortune Wookiee* (2012), *The Surprise Attack of Jabba the Puppet* (2013), *Princess Labelmaker to the Rescue!* (2014), and *Emperor Pickletine Rides the Bus* (2014). There is also a companion activity book titled *ART2-D2's Guide to Folding and Doodling* (2013).

Applegate, Katherine. *Never Glue Your Friends to Chairs* (Roscoe Riley Rules series). Harper, 2008. Gr. 3–4.

First lines: "Hey! Over here! It's me. Roscoe. Welcome to the Official Roscoe Riley Time-Out Corner."

The pitch: Why is Roscoe Riley in time-out? He was just trying to help out his teacher. He says, "How was I supposed to know you shouldn't glue people to chairs? With Super-Mega-Gonzo Glue?" Roscoe goes on to explain, "It's not like I try to find ways to get into trouble. It's just that trouble has a way of finding me." The entire chapter 2 of this book, titled "Something You Should Know before We Get Started," is basically informing us that Super-Mega-Gonzo Glue is permanent, "as in FOREVER AND EVER." The entire chapter 3, titled "Something Else You Should Know before We Get Started," is that gluing things to people is a bad idea. The trouble starts when Roscoe opens his parents' junk drawer. He pulls out a bag of art supplies, three purple rubber bands, a doll head, a "Slinky that wouldn't slink anymore," and a bottle of Super-Mega-Gonzo Glue he takes to school. His class is going to give a performance and sing a song about bees. The kids wear antennae bobbles on their heads, but they keep falling off. Roscoe secretly adds some Super-Mega-Gonzo Glue to each bobble. Just in time for the performance . . .

Reading selection: Read chapter 10, "Bee-Having." Roscoe is worried his classmates won't sit still during their performance. He adds a drop of Super-Mega-Gonzo Glue to each chair. After the performance, the children try to take off their bobbles. Roscoe notices that everyone is starting to look at him. The chapter ends with the lines: "It seemed like maybe a good time for me to go to the bathroom. But when I tried to get up, my chair came with me."

Read-alike recommendations: The series continues with *Never Swipe a Bully's Bear* (2008), *Don't Swap Your Sweater for a Dog* (2008), *Never Swim in Applesauce*

(2008), *Don't Tap-Dance on Your Teacher* (2009), *Never Walk in Shoes That Talk* (2009), and *Never Race a Runaway Pumpkin* (2009).

Gutman, Dan. *Mr. Cooper Is Super!* **(My Weirdest School series). Harper, 2015. Gr. 3–5.**

First line: "My name is A.J., and I hate it when an alien spaceship lands in the middle of the playground."

The pitch: Indeed, an alien spaceship lands in the playground of the Ella Mentry School to whisk the beloved teacher Mr. Granite away. The spaceship is loaded with aliens who all look identical to Mr. Granite; "even the *women* look like Mr. Granite." They've come to return Mr. Granite to his home planet Etinarg, "Granite" spelled backward. A.J. whoops and hollers because he assumes a missing teacher means school will be shut down. The next day, the kids notice they are still without a teacher. A.J. says, "Me and Michael and Ryan did what we always do when there are no grown-ups around. We shook our butts at the class." An adult wearing a superhero outfit falls into the room and announces, "I am *Cooper Man!*"

Reading selection: Read chapter 6. Mr. Cooper insists he has superpowers. When the kids ask him if he can see through walls, Mr. Cooper answers in the affirmative. "Especially walls that have windows in them." He tells them he also has the power to make the kids think about whatever he wants them to think about. He tells them to *not* think of "a pink elephant wearing a tutu and holding a little umbrella while it's singing 'John Jacob Jingleheimer Schmidt.'" Of course, the whole class winds up thinking about the singing pink elephant. They are impressed by Mr. Cooper's superpowers. All except for A.J. who says, "If you ask me, Mr. Cooper is weird."

Read-alike recommendations: The other titles in the series are *Ms. Cuddy Is Nutty!* (2015), *Miss Brown Is Upside Down!* (2015), *Mrs. Meyer Is on Fire!* (2016), and *Miss Daisy Is Still Crazy!* (2016). There are also twenty-one books in the My Weird School series, four editions of My Weird School Special, twelve books in the My Weird School Daze series, and twelve more in the My Weirder School series.

Jennings, Patrick. *Odd, Weird & Little.* **Egmont USA, 2014. Gr. 3–5.**

First line: "The new kid walks in."

The pitch: Woodrow and his classmates are stunned to silence by the appearance of the new kid. He's short and wears a suit and tie, wire-rimmed glasses, a hat, and leather gloves. He carries a briefcase and writes with a bottle of ink and a feather. Woodrow, who up to this point is sometimes picked on as the class weirdo, thinks, "This is an extremely weird kid. Definitely weirder than me. Probably the weirdest in our school. Maybe the weirdest on earth." The new kid's name is Toulouse. Toulouse Hulot. He's from Quebec, Canada, and supposedly speaks very little English. He likes to catch fish and is nervous around cats. A couple of classroom bullies give both Woodrow and Toulouse a hard time. Toulouse handles them expertly and Woodrow gains new self-confidence. As Woodrow continues to observe Toulouse, his thinking shifts a little. "No doubt about it: he's weird. But in a weirdly cool way." The question is—despite the in-your-face-clues the author leaves all over the place—the question is: Who or what is Toulouse?

Reading selection: Read chapter 2, "Weirder Than Woody." The kids are remarking how weird the new kid is. Woodrow finds Toulouse high up in a tree during recess. He tries to make conversation from the ground but has trouble thinking of things to say. He and Toulouse stare at each other. When the school bell rings, Woodrow is surprised to see Toulouse standing next to him on the ground. "The guy was really high. Did he fall? How did he get down so fast?" The school bullies taunt them. When Woodrow whispers to Toulouse to ignore them, Toulouse says his first word: "Who?"

Read-alike recommendations: Author Jennings has another quirky book with *Guinea Dog* (2010), the story of a guinea pig that acts like a dog. There are two more books in that series: *Guinea Dog 2* (2013) and *Guinea Dog 3* (2014).

King, Wesley. *OC Daniel.* Simon & Schuster, 2016. Gr. 5–7.

First line: "I first realized I was crazy on a Tuesday."

The pitch: Thirteen-year-old Daniel Leigh thinks that he's crazy. Or in his words, "bonkers." Daniel has a condition he calls the Zaps. They are bad thoughts or feelings he says makes him feel "like you just got attacked by a Dementor," those creepy flying things from the Harry Potter series. Daniel says, "being Zapped is kind of like heartache. Except heartache doesn't also mean that I think I might die or my little sister might die or I will destroy the entire world if I don't fix the problem. I guess being Zapped is worse." The Zaps make Daniel do crazy things. For example, he's writing a book titled *The Last Kid on Earth*, a book about normal Daniel. It's taking him a while to finish it because he's written the first page fifty-two times and he's "still not happy with it." One of Daniel's classmates is a girl nicknamed Psycho Sara by the other kids. She never talks to anyone. Daniel gets involved in solving the mysterious disappearance of Sara's father. Sara, in turn, helps Daniel learn the true meaning of the Zaps. Here's an example how the Zaps control his life.

Reading selection: Read the first half of chapter 4. Daniel talks about his night Routine. He lists nine steps he has to take to get ready for bed. The Routine consists of steps like, "Wash my hands with ten overlapping squeezes to either hand" and "Flick lights on and off five times." If he messes up one of the routines, he might find himself washing his hands twenty-five times—and crying while doing so—and flicking "lights on and off three hundred and five times." This is a particularly rough night for Daniel. He wakes up from a bad dream. End with the line: "Then I went to go flick the lights."

Read-alike recommendation: The Unlikely Hero of Room 13B by Teresa Toten (Delacorte, 2015) is the story of Adam, a character whose OCD controls his life. Adam joins a support group and all the members take superhero names to help them cope. Adam becomes Batman. *The Unlikely Hero of Room 13B* is for a slightly older audience than *OC Daniel* but is still an easy book for middle schoolers to read.

Krulik, Nancy. *Super Burp!* (George Brown, Class Clown series). Grosset & Dunlap, 2010. Gr. 3–4.

First lines: "Yo George, Never thought I'd say this, but I think it stinks that you won't be going to our school anymore."

The pitch: George hates being the new kid in school. He got into trouble for his pranks at his old school. He's determined to do better at Edith B. Sugarman Elementary (although, in his head, he renames it Edith B. Boogerman Elementary). He is embarrassed when he's introduced to his new fourth-grade class. He feels they are staring at him like he's a two-headed ape. The old George would have acted like an ape and made "ook, ook" noises to get a laugh, but the new George is determined "there would be no ooking at school!" He wants to fit in better with his new classmates, but whispers to himself, "It's not fun not being funny."

Reading selection: Start reading nearly halfway through chapter 5 by repeating the line: "It's not fun not being funny." George is at an ice cream emporium with his parents when they see a shooting star. George makes a wish: "I want to make kids laugh but not get into trouble." He finishes his root beer float when he hears gurgling noises in his belly. "The bubbles bounced up and down and all around. They ping-ponged their way from his belly to his chest, and bing-bonged their way up into his throat. And then . . . B-U-U-U-R-P!" When everyone laughs, something comes over George. He jumps up onto the table, shoves straws up his nose, and shouts, "Look, I'm a walrus." He dances the hokey pokey until all the energy drains out of him. The chapter ends with George thinking, "I'm swearing off root beer floats for good. They're too dangerous."

Read-alike recommendations: The other titles in the series include *Trouble Magnet* (2010), *World's Worst Wedgie* (2010), *What's Black and White and Stinks All Over?* (2011), *Wet and Wild!* (2011), *Help! I'm Stuck in a Giant Nostril!* (2011), *Attack of the Tighty Whities!* (2012), *Hey! Who Stole the Toilet?* (2012), *Dance Your Pants Off!* (2013), *Three Burps and You're Out!* (2013), *Eww! What's on My Shoe?* (2013), *Lice Check* (2014), *How Do You Pee in Space?* (2014), *Snot Funny!* (2015), *A Royal Pain in the Burp* (2015), *Revenge of the Killer Worms* (2015), *It's a Bird, It's a Plane, It's Toiletman!* (2016), and *Dribble, Dribble, Drool!* (2016). George is a spin-off character from the Katie Kazoo series. There are more than thirty titles in that series. The first is *Anyone but Me* (Grosset & Dunlap, 2009).

Look, Lenore. *Alvin Ho: Allergic to Girls, School, and Other Scary Things.* Schwartz & Wade, 2008. Gr. 3–4.

First lines: "The first thing you should know about me is that my name is Alvin Ho. I am afraid of many things."

The pitch: Alvin comes from a long line of Chinese ancestors who weren't afraid of anything. That trait didn't get passed down to Alvin. He lists some of the many, many things he is afraid of. There are the obvious ones like scary movies, the dark, and thunder. He's also afraid of elevators, tunnels, bridges, airplanes, and substitute teachers. Alvin is afraid of school as well. He has never spoken a word in school. He says, "My voice works at home. It works in the car. It even works on the school bus. But as soon as I get to school . . . I am as silent as a side of beef." And now, it's the first day of the new school year.

Reading selection: Read the first part of chapter 2, "Getting—Gulp—Ready for School." Alvin has created a "PDK—Personal Disaster Kit." He includes a whistle, a three-leaf clover (he couldn't find a four-leaf clover), garlic ("for fending off vampires and teachers"), dental floss, a magnifying glass, escape routes, and a scary mask "for keeping girls away." He has written some survival instructions. One of them is titled "How to Meet Your New Teacher" and contains the following steps: "1. Put on a scary mask. 2. Rub on garlic. 3. Stay back 100 feet." His brother Calvin calls Alvin's plans stupid. "Calvin is not supposed to use the s-word, it is bad." Calvin tells Alvin to "look your teacher in the eye, shake her hand and smile." End the passage when Alvin says, "But that's harder than putting on a scary mask."

Read-alike recommendations: Alvin returns in *Alvin Ho: Allergic to Camping, Hiking, and Other Natural Disasters* (2009), *Alvin Ho: Allergic to Birthday Parties, Science Projects, and Other Man-Made Disasters* (2010), *Alvin Ho: Allergic to Dead Bodies, Funerals, and Other Fatal Circumstances* (2011), *Alvin Ho: Allergic to Babies, Burglars, and Other Bumps in the Night* (2013), *Alvin Ho: Allergic to the Great Wall, the Forbidden Palace, and Other Tourist Attractions* (2014).

Pakkala, Christine. *Last-but-Not-Least Lola Going Green.* Boyds Mill, 2013. Gr. 3–4.

First lines: "My name is Lola Zuckerman, and Zuckerman means I'm always last. Just like zippers, zoom, and zebras. Last. Zilch, zeroes, and zombies."

The pitch: Lola is impatient for her teacher Mrs. D to finish the A–Z roll call. Her mom tells her that she should be proud of her last name. "Zuckerman means 'sugar man' in German." Lola retorts, "It means 'last' in Ameri-

can." Mrs. D tells the class they are going to have a Going Green contest. The winner gets to have lunch with Mrs. D in the teacher's lounge. Lola's older brother tells her that the "teacher's lounge is one hundred percent candy." Amanda Anderson used to be Lola's best friend, but they aren't anymore. Lola says, "And it's not because Amanda always gets to go first, in case you think that." These days, the two are like "mustard and pancakes" and "broccoli and cotton candy." When Lola wins the contest (and learns that her brother told her a "ballface lie" about the teacher's lounge), Amanda gets upset and cries. Lola feels terrible. "Seventy-five percent terrible and twenty-five percent not so bad."

Reading selection: Read the last third of chapter 12, "Food Fight!" starting with the sentence: "At lunch I eat far away from Amanda." When Amanda throws her milk carton away, some milk splashes onto Lola. "'Oops,' Amanda says, sweet as pie." Lola squeezes some of her juice box at Amanda, who ducks. "The juice squirts Gwendolyn all over her face." Gwendolyn throws her Smack O Roni 'n Cheese at Lola but it hits Ben. Ben throws his butterscotch pudding and Gwendolyn flips Jamal's tray. The food fight escalates. The principal falls down in a pool of chocolate milk. Amanda and Lola point to each other and each says, "She started it." The chapter ends with the sentence: "And I point at the no-good apple-pie sore loser stinker who rhymes with Pamanda Panderson."

Read-alike recommendations: Lola stars in three more books: *Last-but-Not-Least Lola and the Wild Chicken* (2014), *Last-but-Not-Least Lola and the Cupcake Queen* (2015), and *Last-but-Not-Least Lola and a Knot the Size of Texas* (2016).

Van Draanen, Wendelin. *Secret Identity* (Shredderman series). Knopf, 2004. Gr. 3–5.

First line: "Bubba Bixby was born big and mean, full of teeth and ready to bite."

The pitch: The school bully Bubba also has "rocky knuckles" and "killer breath." One time, Bubba shouted at a third grader and the kid's "eyes rolled up in his head. His knees buckled. Then he blacked out and hit the dirt." That's how bad Bubba's breath is. He also lies, cheats, and takes things from his classmates. The only things Bubba gives his classmates are new names, names like "Moron," "Butthead," and "Worm Lips." Nolan Byrd is nicknamed Byrd-the-Nerd" and he doesn't like it one bit. In fact, Nolan decides to fight back through the Internet. He creates a new identity for himself—Shredderman. He was inspired after a teacher paid him a compliment by writing, *"Nolan—You shred, man! Awesome!"* Shredderman's power is to fight for truth and justice. Nolan secretly records Bubba lying, cheating, and stealing and posts these recordings on a new website: Shredderman.com. The site becomes very popular, making Bubba very, very angry.

Reading selection: Read the second half of chapter 6, "Building the Site." Start with the sentence: "Welcome to Shredderman.com, where truth and justice prevail!" Nolan adds "Bubba jokes" like "Why run from a bully? He's got the Bub-onic plague." It has a link called "Bubba's Big Butt" with a picture of Bubba's rear end. An additional link asks: "What's big and fat and smells all over?" and returns to the same picture of Bubba's butt. The chapter ends with Nolan going through his checklist. "I wasn't tired—I was wired! Wired, and ready to *shred.*"

Read-alike recommendations: There are three more books in the series: *Attack of the Tagger* (2004), *Meet the Gecko* (2005), and *Enemy Spy* (2005).

CHAPTER 15

Books about Kids Who Hate to Read

This final category is where I say, "And if reluctant readers haven't been hooked by any other format or genre, then perhaps they'd like to read about another kid who either hates reading in general or hates the choices teachers, librarians, and parents present to them."

Alexander, Kwame. *Booked.* Houghton Mifflin Harcourt, 2016. Gr. 5–7.
First lines: "on the pitch, lightning fa**S**t, / dribble, fake, then make a dash / player tries t**O** steal the ball / lift and step and make him fall."

The pitch: Eighth grader Nick Hall is very bright (he skipped a grade) but is not much interested in school. Nick lets everyone know that he hates words. His father has written a unique dictionary and Nick is forced to read it. He wishes his father was a musician or a "cool detective / driving / a sleek silver / convertible sports car / like Will Smith / in *Bad Boys.*" Nick resists the efforts of Mr. Mac, the school librarian and a former rap star, and his book recommendations. He also thinks his English honors class "is one boring / required read / after another." Nick's fed up having adults tell him what to read. When his parents separate, he thinks about his life. "If not for soccer, / what'd be the point?"

Reading selection: Read a series of poems, beginning "Ever since first grade." We meet Nick's best friend Coby and learn they play on different teams. "The most dangerous player / on the rival soccer club / also happens to be / your best friend." Move on to "Best Friend." "Coby Lee / is from Singapore. Sorta. / He was born there, like his dad, but / his mom's from Ghana." His room is plastered with posters of soccer teams from both areas but "unfortunately, / you rarely see / any of this / because / your best friend's room / always smells / like skunk pee / and funky freakin' / feet." Continue to read the one-page-length poems "Braggin' Rights" and "The Letter" and conclude with the poem "Dad's back in town" and its last line: "*I hate books.*"

Read-alike recommendation: Author Alexander also wrote the novel-in-verse book *The Crossover* (2014), featuring two basketball-playing brothers.

Colfer, Eoin. *Legend of Spud Murphy.* Hyperion, 2004. Gr. 3–5.

First lines: "I've got four brothers. Imagine that. Five boys under eleven all living in the same house."

The pitch: Will, the nine-year-old narrator, and Marty, his ten-year-old brother, get blamed for everything. The three youngest brothers never get blamed for anything. "Donnie, Bert, and HP could stick an ax in my head and they'd still get off with ten minutes no TV and a stern look." Their parents exile the two oldest brothers to spend their afternoons at the public library. Will says, "I'd much rather be outside riding a horse than inside reading about one." The boys plead that the library is a dangerous place because the head librarian, Mrs. Murphy, has a spud gun—a gun that shoots potatoes. The kids all call her Spuds Murphy because she supposedly shoots potatoes at misbehaving kids. The boys are still forced to go to the library. Will says the books are "just waiting to jump off the shelves and bore me silly." Mrs. Murphy warns the boys to stay on the carpet in the juvenile section "or there will be trouble." Marty tests Spuds by rearranging the books, placing them on the wrong shelves.

Reading selection: Begin halfway through chapter 3, "The Test," with the sentence: "Suddenly, a shadow fell across my brother." Mrs. Murphy "appeared without a sound, like a ninja librarian." Spuds nails Marty with a book stamp, and "two hours and fourteen paper cuts later," Marty has to put all the books back in their proper place. When Spud asks Marty if he'd like a temporary tattoo of a pirate, she places a Barbie tattoo on his arm. She says, "Oops." The chapter ends with Spud calling to Marty, "Enjoy swimming."

Read-alike recommendations: Will and Marty return in *Legend of Captain Crow's Teeth* (2005) and *Legend of the Worst Boy in the World* (2007).

Gifford, Peggy. *Moxy Maxwell Does Not Love Stuart Little.* Schwartz & Wade, 2007. Gr. 3–5.

First line: "Her name was Moxy Maxwell and she was nine and it was August and late August at that."

The pitch: Tomorrow is the first day of school. Moxy did not finish—did not even start—her summer reading assignment. Her assignment was to read the book *Stuart Little.* "Moxy settled back and considered the curious fact that she had preferred cleaning her room to reading a book. It was peculiar because Moxy hated cleaning her room." In fact, this whole book is how Moxy avoids reading *Stuart Little.* Chapter 3 is almost as short as the chapter's title, "In Which We Get Back to the Point." Chapter 7, titled "In Which Moxy's Mother Says No," consists of only one word. Moxy has good intentions. She carries her copy of the book in her backpack, she sticks it under the broken coffee table leg, and it even goes for a swim in the pool with her.

Reading selection: Read chapter 4, "'Just in Case of In-Between' Explained." Moxy thinks she can get some reading in "just in case one thing ends before the next thing begins." She tries to explain to her mother that "my in-betweens are always interrupted by other things." She recounts the time she started reading *Stuart Little* and her glass of lemonade spilled all over the book. "A billion ants came the next day." The chapter ends with Moxy explaining, "That's what I mean about being interrupted every time I have an in-between."

Read-alike recommendations: Moxy returns in *Moxy Maxwell Does Not Love Writing Thank-You Notes* (2008) and *Moxy Maxwell Does Not Love Practicing the Piano (But She Does Love Being in Recitals)* (2009).

Greenwald, Tommy. *Charlie Joe Jackson's Guide to Not Reading.* Roaring Brook, 2011. Gr. 4–7.

First lines: "My name is Charlie Joe Jackson, and I hate reading. And if you're reading this book, you hate reading, too."

The pitch: Charlie says it in the very first chapter. "I hate reading." He goes on to say that his book will help anyone get out of reading and, yes, he points out the irony of the fact one has to read his book to learn how to avoid reading books. Charlie is no quitter. He's committed to not reading. He shares plenty of tips. For example, Charlie states that if a book was turned into a movie, rent the movie. With another helpful tip, Charlie suggests picking a book with short chapters. One of Charlie's chapters is one sentence long, with only three words. Chapter 27 reads: "There, that's better." Here are some more of Charlie's tips. . . .

Reading selection: Read "Charlie Joe's Tip #3." It contains ten tips on how to get out of reading. The tips include feeding your book to the dog. Move on to the second page of chapter 14, beginning with the sentence: "I knew something was wrong right when I got home, when I walked in the door and Moose and

Coco didn't run up to greet me as if I was the only human being in the world that had ever existed." Charlie's mother is sitting with Ms. Rose McGibney, the mother of his former best friend Timmy. Charlie's mother says, "Rose has come here today with some very disturbing news." The chapter ends with Charlie asking the reader if they want to learn more, or put the book away and watch TV. Charlie makes the decision for us and ends with the lines: "That settles it. End of chapter."

Read-alike recommendations: Charlie returns in *Charlie Joe Jackson's Guide to Extra Credit* (2012),

Charlie Joe Jackson's Guide to Summer Vacation (2013), *Charlie Joe Jackson's Guide to Making Money* (2014), *Charlie Joe Jackson's Guide to Planet Girl* (2015), and *Charlie Joe Jackson's Guide to Growing Up* (2016). There are three spin-off titles with characters from the Charlie Joe books: *Jack Strong Takes a Stand* (2013), *Katie Friedman Gives Up Texting! (And Lives to Tell about It)* (2015), and *Pete Milano's Guide to Being a Movie Star* (2016).

Tashjian, Janet. *My Life as a Book*. Holt, 2010. Gr. 4–7.
   First line: "I DON'T WANT TO READ THIS BOOK!"
   The pitch: Derek doesn't hate to read, exactly. He just doesn't want to read books that adults want him to read. "If everyone just left me alone with Calvin, Hobbes, Garfield, Bucky, and Satchel, I could read all day." He thinks that "maybe it's like blue eyes and blond hair—there's a reading gene some people get or don't get at birth." Derek does like to draw. His drawings appear in the margins of this book. Instead of reading books, Derek would rather put action figures under the tires of eighteen-wheelers to see them squash like grapes or get his head purposely caught in the car's side window. He has to read not one, not two, but three assigned books for his teacher over the summer. Derek gets sidetracked by the mysterious drowning death of a girl that happened ten years earlier and somehow involves his family. Derek's summer goes from "being the best season to the absolute total worst."
   Reading selection: Read the chapter titled "A New Friend." Derek's mother is a veterinarian and one day she is checking Pedro, a monkey "trained to work with people in wheelchairs." When his mother isn't looking, Derek sneaks Pedro to his basement and dresses him in a cowboy outfit with a toy gun. He then places the monkey on the back of his dog, Bodi. "Either he wants Pedro off his back or he's willing to play along, because Bodi takes off through the house with Pedro holding on to his collar for dear life. Bodi is barking and Pedro's shrieking, so I start screaming, too and grab the gun that Pedro dropped. The three of us race through the house when I suddenly see my mother standing in the doorway." This is apparently the last straw because his mother informs him that because of his behavior, Derek gets to spend the rest of the summer at Learning Camp. The chapter ends with a bummed Derek thinking, "Why can't grown-ups just let a kid play with a dog and a monkey in peace?"
   Read-alike recommendations: Derek also appears in *My Life as a Stuntboy* (2011), *My Life as a Cartoonist* (2013), *My Life as a Joke* (2014), and *My Life as a Gamer* (2015).

References

Anderson, Richard C., Elfrieda H. Hiebert, Judith A. Scott, and Ian A. G. Wilkinson. 1985. *Becoming a Nation of Readers*. Champaign-Urbana: University of Illinois, Center for the Study of Reading.

Baker, Linda, and Allan Wigfield. 1999. "Dimension of Children's Motivation for Reading and Their Relations to Reading Activity and Reading Achievement." *Reading Research Quarterly* 34:452–78.

Benning, Katy. 2014. "Independent Reading: Shifting Reluctant Readers to Authentic Engagement in the Middle Level." *Journal of Adolescent & Adult Literacy* 57:632.

Brinda, Wayne. 2011. "A 'Ladder to Literacy' Engages Reluctant Readers." *Middle School Journal* 43:8–17.

Ciesla, Katie. 2016. "Reaching Reluctant Readers through Read-Aloud." *The Reading Teacher* 69:523.

Crowe, Chris. 1999. "Rescuing Reluctant Readers." *English Journal* 88:113–16.

Erickson, Barbara. 1996. "Read-Alouds Reluctant Readers Relish." *Journal of Adolescent & Adult Literacy* 40:212–14.

Gutchewsky, Kimberly. 2001. "An Attitude Adjustment: How I Reached My Reluctant Readers." *The English Journal* 91:79–85.

Jobe, Ron, and Mary Dayton-Sakari. 1999. *Reluctant Readers: Connecting Students and Books for Successful Reading Experiences*. Markham, ON: Pembroke.

Nielen, Thijs M.J., Suzanne E. Mol, Maria T. Sikkema-de Jong, and Adriana Bus. 2016. "Attentional Bias toward Reading in Reluctant Readers." *Contemporary Educational Psychology* 46:263–71.

Trelease, Jim. 2013. *The Read-Aloud Handbook*. 7th ed. New York: Penguin.

YALSA (Young Adult Library Services Association). 2016. "Quick Picks for Reluctant Young Adult Readers Selection Criteria." Last modified 2016. http://www.ala.org/yalsa/booklistsawards/booklists/quickpicks/quickpicksreluctantyoung.

Further Reading

Allyn, Pam. 2009. *What to Read When: The Books and Stories to Read with Your Child—and All the Best Times to Read Them.* New York: Penguin.

Baxter, Kathleen A., and Marcia Agness Kochel. 2008. *Gotcha Good! Nonfiction Books to Get Kids Excited about Reading.* Westport, CT: Libraries Unlimited.

Foote, Diane. 2014. *Popular Picks for Young Readers.* Chicago: ALA Editions.

Keane, Nancy J. 2012. *101 Great, Ready-to-Use Book Lists for Children.* Westport, CT: Libraries Unlimited.

Miller, Donalyn. 2009. *The Book Whisperer: Awakening the Inner Reader in Every Child.* San Francisco: Jossey-Bass.

Reid, Rob. 2009. *Reid's Read-Alouds: Selections for Children and Teens.* Chicago: ALA Editions.

———. 2010. *Reid's Read-Alouds 2: Modern Day Classics from C. S. Lewis to Lemony Snicket.* Chicago: ALA Editions.

———. 2012. *Silly Books to Read Aloud.* Chicago: Huron Street.

———. 2014. *Biographies to Read Aloud with Kids.* Chicago: Huron Street.

Sullivan, Michael. 2014. *Raising Boy Readers.* Chicago: Huron Street.

Index

About the Author

Rob Reid teaches children's and young adult literature courses at the University of Wisconsin, Eau Claire (UWEC). He is a former junior high school English teacher, a youth services librarian for both the Pueblo, Colorado, Library District and the L. E. Phillips Memorial Public Library in Eau Claire, Wisconsin, and a youth services/special needs consultant for the Indianhead Federated Library System. He is the author of two picture books and eighteen literature resource books, including *Reid's Read-Alouds: Selections for Children and Teens*, *Reid's Read-Alouds 2: Modern-Day Classics from C. S. Lewis to Lemony Snicket*, *Biographies to Read Aloud with Kids*, and *Silly Books to Read Aloud*. Rob has written more than one hundred journal articles for *American Libraries*, *School Library Journal*, and *LibrarySparks* magazine, and he has an ongoing column in *Book Links* magazine titled the Reid-Aloud Alert.

Rob's awards include the 2004 Wisconsin Librarian of the Year, the 2007 Lucy Beck Storytelling Award for best storyteller in Wisconsin, the 2009 Ron Satz Teacher/Scholar Award for UWEC, the 2013 Children's Legacy Outstanding Achievement Award sponsored by the Eau Claire Community Foundation, and the 2016 Jeff Oliphant Blugold Spirit Award for UWEC.

When Rob is not teaching, writing, or reading, he is playing with his four grandchildren and hiking in the woods with his wife, Jayne.